About Richard Webster

Author of over seventy-five books, Richard Webster is one of New Zealand's most prolific authors. His best-selling books include *Spirit Guides and Angel Guardians* and *Creative Visualization for Beginners*, and he is also the author of *Soul Mates, Is Your Pet Psychic?, Practical Guide to Past-Life Memories, Astral Travel for Beginners, Miracles*, and the four-book series on archangels *Michael, Gabriel, Raphael*, and *Uriel*.

A noted psychic, Richard is a member of the National Guild of Hypnotherapists (USA), the Association of Professional Hypnotherapists and Parapsychologists (UK), the International Registry of Professional Hypnotherapists (Canada), and the Psychotherapy and Hypnotherapy Institute of New Zealand. When not touring, he resides in New Zealand with his wife and family.

To Write to the Author

If you wish to contact the author or would like more information about this book, please write to the author in care of Llewellyn Worldwide and we will forward your request. Both the author and publisher appreciate hearing from you and learning of your enjoyment of this book and how it has helped you. Llewellyn Worldwide cannot guarantee that every letter written to the author can be answered, but all will be forwarded. Please write to:

Richard Webster
℅ Llewellyn Worldwide
2143 Wooddale Drive, Dept. 978-0-7387-1349-6
Woodbury, MN 55125-2989, U.S.A.

Please enclose a self-addressed stamped envelope for a reply,
or $1.00 to cover costs. If outside the U.S.A., enclose an
international postal reply coupon.

Many of Llewellyn's authors have websites with additional information and resources. For more information, please visit our website at http://www.llewellyn.com.

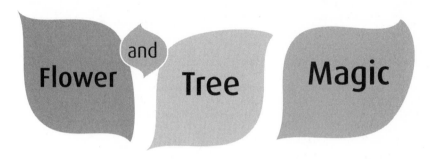

Flower and Tree Magic

Discover the Natural Enchantment Around You

Richard Webster

Llewellyn Publications
Woodbury, Minnesota

First Edition
First Printing, 2008

Book design by Steffani Sawyer
Editing by Brett Fechheimer
Cover art © 2008 by Pixtal/Art Life Images
Cover design by Lisa Novak
Llewellyn is a registered trademark of Llewellyn Worldwide, Ltd.

Library of Congress Cataloging-in-Publication Data

Webster, Richard, 1946–
   Flower and tree magic: discover the natural enchantment around you / Richard Webster. — 1st ed.
      p. cm.
   Includes bibliographical references and index.
   ISBN 978-0-7387-1349-6
   1. Flowers—Psychic aspects. 2. Trees—Psychic aspects. I. Title.
   BF1045.P55W43 2008
   133'.258213—dc22
                              2008009555

Llewellyn Publications
A Division of Llewellyn Worldwide, Ltd.
2143 Wooddale Drive, Dept. 978-0-7387-1349-6
Woodbury, Minnesota 55125-2989, U.S.A.
www.llewellyn.com

Printed in the United States of America

Other Books by Richard Webster

For my goddaughter
Alice Pope
with love

Contents

Contents

Introduction

*T*he inspiration for this book came from an elderly lady I used to chat with every time I walked past her house. She had a beautiful garden and tended it with love. No matter what time of year it was, something was flowering, as she believed color was healing and restorative to the soul.

"Flowers are magical," Cynthia told me. "They have a profound effect on our psyches. I'd have been dead years ago if it hadn't been for my flowers. I benefit from choosing them, planting them, nurturing them, and looking at them. They enhance every aspect of my life."

Her mention of the magical effect of flowers intrigued me. I began using flowers more frequently in my rituals and divinations, and found them extremely helpful. I also noticed the effect they had on my clients. Without exception, everyone was enthusiastic and encouraged me to explore this field further.

Flowers have always played an important role in everyday life. They are used to celebrate special occasions such as weddings and anniversaries. They are given as a token of love, especially on Valentine's Day and Mother's Day. They are even used as a sign of respect and remembrance at funerals. Flowers relate to us at a deep, emotional level.

Plants have always been used in magic. Corn is arguably the first plant to be used in this way. It symbolized the end of winter and the welcome return of spring. It also, in a very real sense, signified the creation of food.

Mandrake has been used in magic for thousands of years, probably because its roots frequently resemble a human figure. Mandrake is also a narcotic, and people used it to relieve aches and pains and as a cure for depression.

Laurel was used by the ancient Greeks to enter an altered state. It was chewed or smoked to achieve the desired effect. Many of the famous Greek oracles used laurel.

Plants were used to protect people from witches and the effects of the evil eye. One remedy was to wear a garland of bittersweet.

Some plants were considered unlucky. Even today it is considered unlucky to bring blackthorn or hawthorn into the house. Belladonna, or deadly nightshade, was extremely unlucky. It was also highly poisonous, and people believed witches made an ointment from it that enabled them to fly. Witches were also believed to use ragwort to help them fly.

Witches' brooms were known as besoms. They were made from stalks of broom or birch tied to a stick. Twigs of heather were sometimes used.

Henbane was considered a highly magical plant, and was made into a variety of love potions. The smoke produced when it was burned enabled witches to conjure up evil spirits and gaze into the future. Herbalists also used henbane as a painkiller.

Fairies were also believed to use flowers to achieve their ends. Foxglove is sometimes referred to as "fairy weed." Bare circles of soil were known as "fairy rings," and people believed they were caused by fairies dancing around in a circle. Fairy rings brought luck to neighboring buildings, but it was considered highly dangerous to step inside one.

Plants have always played a major role in love magic. The four-leaf clover is a good example. If a young girl found a four-leaf clover and placed it in her right shoe, the next single man she met would become her husband.

Flowers have always been used to convey secret messages. The ultimate example of flowers being used in this way was the language of flowers, which we'll discuss in chapter 8.

Trees were considered sacred in many parts of the world. Individual trees were believed to possess magical properties.

One of the greatest benefits of tree and flower magic is that it brings people closer to nature. Herbs, flowers, and trees have always provided humankind with medicine for the body and beauty for the soul. Much of this has been lost in modern times, although it's interesting to notice a resurgence of interest in what used to be considered "old-fashioned" remedies.

It is still possible to grow a magical garden today, even if you do not have a garden. I know several people who grow herbs and magical flowers in pots and window boxes. You might want to grow St. John's wort, one of the most famous magical flowers of all. If you pick the flowers on Midsummer's Eve you will attract love and good luck. Yellow is the color of the sun, and St. John's wort is a good example of a flower that reflects the generosity and good fortune provided by the sun. Other examples include marigolds, the heliotrope, and of course, the sunflower.

If you need more money, you should plant flowers that relate to Jupiter, the planet of expansion and prosperity. Lilac and honeysuckle are good examples.

If you need more virility and passion in your life, plant some red flowers. These relate to Mars. Blue flowers relate to Venus and will help you in matters concerning love and romance. Roses of all colors relate to Venus, but the best ones for love purposes are the pink and red varieties, especially the stronger-scented ones.

You will need some white flowers in your garden, too, as these represent the moon. Solomon's seal and lilies are good examples. You can attract good luck by cutting white flowers on the day of the new moon and displaying them in an attractive vase near a window, where the moon's rays can shine on them.

one

Sacred and Magical Trees

*C*ertain trees have always been considered magical and sacred. The myths and folklore of northern Europe are full of stories that involve the powerful spiritual presence provided by trees. Trees are full of the energy and life force provided by Mother Earth. At one time, tree worship was extremely common. People who lived in forested areas observed the mysterious growth of trees, and believed it to be caused by the spirits who lived inside them. Trees were thought to be the homes of the gods, and the rustling of the leaves spoke an otherworldly message. Trees were rooted in the earth but reached up into heaven. The mystery of trees that shed their leaves in autumn, and produced beautiful new leaves in spring, symbolized rebirth and renewal. Evergreen trees symbolized the universal, everlasting spirit. The superstition of knocking on wood for luck dates all the way back to ancient tree worship.

Trees provided shelter and shade, and timber provided heat and building materials. Amulets and talismans were made from their wood, and they were planted in strategic positions to provide protection from the forces of evil. The fruits, flowers, leaves, and roots provided food and medicine. People gained energy and emotional healing by walking through a forest or grove of trees.

The ancient Canaanites deified the tree. Tree trunks were shorn of their branches and erected for worship. These trunks were sacred to the goddess Asherah and shared her name. Chips or splinters taken from an asherah were prized and sought after, as they bestowed fertility and abundance. The saying "a chip off the old block" comes from this belief.[1]

There is even an apparent reference to the magical and spiritual aspects of trees in the Bible. Genesis 21:33 reads: "And Abraham planted a grove in Beersheba, and called there on the name of the Lord, the everlasting God."

---

1. Rudolph Brasch, *Strange Customs: How Did They Begin?* (New York: McKay, 1976), 171.

The ancient Celts venerated the oak, ash, and thorn, believing the trio to be an extremely powerful and sacred combination. Groves containing all three of these are particularly magical places. Many people have claimed to see fairies while resting or meditating in a grove containing the triad of ash, oak, and thorn.

The English tell a charming legend about Joseph of Arimathea. When he arrived at Glastonbury in 63 CE, he planted his staff in the ground on Wearyall Hill and it immediately blossomed into a hawthorn tree. This tree, known as the Holy Thorn, bloomed every Christmas. A Puritan cut it down in 1643, but fortunately its descendants survived and bloom to this day. A new Holy Thorn was planted on the hill in 1951.

The maypole dance, still performed in many English villages on the first day of May each year, is derived from ancient fertility rituals. Traditionally, people gathered flowers and greenery to help celebrate this day and to bring fertility to the entire community. Originally, people danced around a hawthorn tree, but over time this was superseded by a pole garlanded with flowers.

The burning of the yule log at Christmas was originally performed to encourage the sun to return and create spring. The yule log is almost always oak.

The Tree of Life appears in many creation mythologies, including those of the Zoroastrians, Babylonians, and Egyptians. The belief is that the world is flat and a large tree supports the heavens above.

The Yakut of Siberia tell the story of the first man who set out to explore the world. He came across a huge tree that joined heaven, Earth, and the Underworld. The spirit of the tree used its leaves to communicate with the gods. The first man was lonely and asked the tree for help. The spirit of the tree caused a young woman to emerge from beneath its roots. She offered him milk from her breasts, and immediately the man was filled with confidence, strength, and energy.[2]

The Tree of Life mentioned in the Bible (Genesis 2:9 and 3:22) conferred immortality. People sometimes confuse this tree with the one from which Adam and Eve ate. That tree is called the Tree of Knowledge of Good and Evil. Of course, once Adam and Eve had been expelled from the Garden of Eden they left the Tree of Life behind, which meant they were no longer immortal.

Stories of this sort show just how magical trees were to ancient people.

Pre-Columbian cultures saw the world in much the same way. A silk cotton or kapok tree, known as the World Tree, rose from the Underworld and ascended to the heavens. The Mayans believed the souls of the dead climbed this tree to get to heaven. The souls of people who committed suicide rested in the shade of the World Tree, and were protected by the goddess Ixtab.

The ancient Chinese also worshipped trees. Chinese mythology includes a number of huge trees that connect heaven and Earth. People are able to climb them to get to heaven, but to proceed further they need to gain the approval of the guardian deities who sit at the top of the tree. The leaning mulberry tree was one of the most important of these. In Chinese mythology, ten suns rose from the mulberry tree and caused a drought that threatened the entire world. Fortunately, a famous archer named Yu killed nine of the suns with his arrows, and thus saved the entire world from disaster.

Another important tree in Chinese lore is the peach, known as the Tree of Life. It was one of seven trees that grew on the slopes of the Kuen-Luèn Mountains. The goddess Si Wang Mu gave gifts of peaches to people, and anyone who received one became immortal. The peach blossoms in February, considered a good time of the year for weddings. Even today the Chinese consider the peach to

---

2. Brian Leigh Molyneaux and Piers Vitebsky, *Sacred Earth, Sacred Stones* (San Diego, CA: Laurel Glen Publishing, 2001), 83.

be a symbol of longevity, immortality, and a happy marriage.[3] Chinese artists frequently show the God of Long Life emerging from a ripe peach.

Trees were frequently decorated with garlands and lanterns as part of tree worship. Shrines were often placed in the fork of a tree, as this is where local gods lived. A strip of red cloth was sometimes attached to the tree to protect it and ward off evil spirits.

In Scandinavia, Yggdrasil was a huge ash tree at the center of the world. Its roots went all the way down to the Underworld, its trunk was in the world of humans, and its branches were up in the heavens. A famous story tells how Odin hung himself upside down on this tree for nine nights in order to gain wisdom, understanding, and knowledge of the runes.

In Bali, the banyan tree is believed to connect heaven and Earth.

The Tree of Life is also the name given to the diagram of the Kabbalah, which was originally depicted as a tree.

The Dyak tribes in Borneo have a Tree of Life called *Kayu Abilau*, which can be climbed by dream-wanderers when they are in a trance state. Once they have climbed the tree, they can talk to Aping, their god of the forest.[4]

Various mythologies tell how mankind was created from trees. In Norse mythology, Odin and his brothers created the first man, Askr, from an ash tree, and his wife, Embla, from an elm. In the Greek tradition, Zeus used the trunks of ash trees to create the bronze men.

A tribe of Australian aborigines called the Yarralin has a grove of trees near Lingara, in the Northern Territory, which is used for sacred dreaming. Young men gather clay from the billabong, or

3. H. T. Morgan, *Chinese Symbols and Superstitions* (South Pasadena, CA: P. D. Perkins and Ione Perkins, 1942), 111.

4. Rowena and Rupert Shepherd, *1000 Symbols* (London: Thames and Hudson, 2002), 236.

water hole, in the middle of the grove and mix it with scrapings of bark from the trees to make a potion they believe will help them attract women. Their womenfolk also have dreaming trees, and visit them to receive the necessary spiritual essence to stimulate conception and birth.

Many trees have been considered sacred and magical at different times. Here are some of the most important of them:

Alder

The alder tree burns easily and has been called the tree of fire. In the Greek tradition, the alder was sacred to Phoroneus, the inventor of fire. In Celtic mythology, the alder is extremely brave and fought in the front line during the battle of the trees. Whistles made from alder wood are reputed to be able to harness and control the four winds. Flutes can also be made from alder and used for magical purposes. Herbalists in Europe prescribed alder bark to treat inflammations. Heated alder leaves were used to treat chronic skin problems, and the bark and leaves were used to create a gargle to relieve mouth ulcers.

Almond

The almond tree has been considered the tree of wisdom ever since Jeremiah saw an almond branch in a vision (Jeremiah 1:11). This branch symbolized the gift of prophecy and wisdom that God gave to Jeremiah.

Moses took twelve rods from different families into the tabernacle, and Aaron's rod was made of almond wood. While in the tabernacle it budded, blossomed, and produced almonds (Numbers 17:8). This signified that Aaron and his descendants would become the religious leaders of the Jewish people.

The ancient Aramaic name for almond is *luz*, which means "light." This is because they believed divine light shone mystically from the almond. Jacob experienced his famous dream while staying at Luz, an almond grove in Canaan (Genesis 28:11–19). This divine light is still represented in the menorah today, which contains a light for all seven planets.

In the Christian tradition, the almond symbolizes divine grace and is associated with the Virgin Mary. In Persia, the almond symbolized the tree of heaven. In China, the almond symbolizes femininity and the necessary strength to surmount difficult situations.

The almond tree is popular with fairies who enjoy its sweetness and modest nature.

Apple

The apple tree was sacred to the Druids. Apple was considered a tree of choice, since meditating under it would help one make the correct decision. Magic wands are frequently made from apple wood. The Druids associated it with fertility and marriage.

The apple has been associated with health, passion, and earthly pleasures since the time of the ancient Greeks. The Greeks dedicated the apple to Demeter, goddess of sustenance, and Aphrodite, goddess of love.

Many people assume the forbidden fruit that Eve gave to Adam was an apple. However, the Bible refers to it only as fruit from the "tree of the knowledge of good and evil" (Genesis 2:17).

If you cut an apple in half horizontally to the stem, the core forms a pentagram, a sacred figure in magic. The fruit of the apple is frequently used in spells and potions to attract love. In fairy tales, the eating of an apple virtually guaranteed a young couple would be blessed with children. During the Renaissance, young Frenchmen tried to capture the hearts of young maidens by offering them an apple. In medieval Germany, young men carved letters into an apple before giving it to their girlfriends to eat. An old Italian story tells how a pig accidentally ate one of these apples and fell madly in love with the young man who had carved letters into it.

Not long ago I saw a young woman twisting the stem of an apple while calling out the letters of the alphabet. She was following an ancient ritual that says the stem will break when she calls out the first letter of the name of her future lover.

A close friend of mine, who regularly communicates with trees, insists the apple tree is the happiest, friendliest tree of all. It enjoys providing a bountiful crop of fruit for people who look after it.

An old English custom says that people can help apple trees produce bountiful crops over many years by drinking cider under them and offering them a toast.

Pruned branches from an apple tree can be burned in a fireplace to bring good luck to everyone living in the home. For best results, soak the branches in brine or seawater for a lunar month (twenty-eight days). Allow the branches to dry out completely and then enjoy the pleasant odor they produce while burning.

The story of John Chapman (1774–1845), better known as Johnny Appleseed, has become an integral part of American culture. His mission in life was to grow and distribute apple trees. He collected seeds from cider presses in Pennsylvania and carried them west on horseback. He sold his trees for a "flip penny bit" (about six cents) but also accepted used clothing and promissory notes as payment. He also gave away trees to farmers who could not afford to buy them. His generosity, eccentric appearance, and cheerful personality all contributed to the legend that grew up about him. The words on his tombstone read: "He lived for others."

Ash

The ash has been considered a sacred tree for thousands of years. An ancient Norse tradition claims that the first man was created from the branches of an ash tree. (The same tradition says the first woman was created from an elm.) The ash is sometimes referred to as the tree of knowledge. The Celts considered it a tree of enchantment, and Druids made healing wands from its branches. The ancient Greeks carried pieces of ash with them as lucky charms when traveling over water. This was because ash was considered sacred to Poseidon, the god of the ocean.

An ash leaf containing an even number of leaflets is considered extremely fortunate and is still sometimes used as a charm to attract love. If you place the leaf under your pillow, you will dream of your future lover. Unfortunately, ash leaves with an even number of leaflets are extremely rare. Young women had to recite a rhyme when they found one:

> This even ash I double in three,
> The first man I meet my true love shall be;
> If he be married let him pass by,
> But if he be single, let him draw nigh.

Banyan

The banyan tree (*Ficus bengalensis*) has always been one of the most sacred trees in Asia. It is connected to Brahma, the immortal spirit or essence of the universe. Consequently, in India the banyan tree symbolizes immortality. The banyan tree is also considered remarkable, since it keeps on growing no matter how many of its branches are cut. The banyan is also related to people who grow and develop spiritually. Nowadays, people still water the roots and place offerings on banyan trees to attract good luck, happiness, and fertility.

See also *Bodhi*.

Beech

Until the Iron Age, the beech was a valuable source of food for people—who ate its leaf buds, leaves, and nuts. Oil was extracted from the nuts and provided an excellent source of protein.

The beech has also given us the word *book*, as slices of beech were bound together and written on to preserve knowledge.

Beech provides good luck and protection. It is an excellent wood for magic wands and lucky charms. At one time, the bark of the beech tree was used as a remedy for fever and to reduce swelling.

Birch

The birch has always symbolized fertility and new life. Jumping the broomstick, which is made of birch, is still a popular pagan tradition. In Britain, single women would sometimes give their boyfriends a twig of birch to encourage them to propose.

In Norse mythology, the birch is associated with Freya, the lady of the forest. This is taken even further in Russia, where the birch tree itself is called Lady of the Forest.

Birch twigs are used to drive away evil spirits and to encourage the spirits of the previous year to leave. Today birch twigs are still used on the body in saunas and sweat lodges to stimulate circulation.

Birch wood can be used in any rituals or spells involving cleansing, support, or protection.

Traditionally, the three most fortunate trees to have close to home are the maple, the oak, and the silver birch. Folklore says that an oak tree will usually be found close to a birch tree, as they are considered husband and wife.

Bodhi

The bodhi tree is a species of fig. Hindus and Buddhists consider the bodhi tree to be the tree of wisdom. More than 2,600 years ago, Siddhartha Gautama achieved nirvana, or divine enlightenment, under a pipal tree (*Ficus religiosa*) at Bodh Gaya in northeastern India, and became Buddha. The sacred tree that Buddha used for shelter became known as *bo* or *bodhi*, which means "the tree of awakening." Pilgrims still visit this sacred sanctuary today and can meditate under trees that are direct descendants of the tree Buddha used.

Cedar

The cedar tree was associated with fertility and immortality. Its wood was believed to be indestructible. For that reason, the cedar is commonly used to provide protection. The cedar was sacred to the Phoenicians and Sumerians. The Sumerians considered the cedar to be the World Tree, and the home of Ea, the creator of all humanity. The Chaldeans believed the cedar held all the secrets to the mystery of life.

The Egyptians used cedar oil for embalming purposes. The Celts also used cedar oil to preserve the heads of enemies killed in battle.

Because the most important gods lived inside cedar trees, the trees were asked if they could be used in the construction of temples. It was especially important to have cedar doors, as the tree was a door to the divine and the door to a temple also symbolized the entrance to the divine. King Solomon's temple contained a large amount of cedar, including the ceiling (1 Kings 6:15). King David's house was built entirely from cedar (2 Samuel 7:2). The cedars of Lebanon are mentioned several times in the Bible (Judges 9:15; Psalms 92:12, 104:16, 148:9; Solomon 5:15; Isaiah 2:13; Ezekiel 17:3).

Cherry

The cherry blossom is the national flower of Japan. Samurai warriors meditated upon the meaning of life and death while sitting under cherry trees. This is because the cherry blossom fell to the ground and died while apparently at its peak of blossoming.

Elsewhere, the cherry has sexual overtones. In China, to say "eating cherries" is a hidden way of saying "sexual intercourse." In the West, the term "losing one's cherry" indicates a woman has lost her virginity. This is because the cherry is associated with the hymen.

Eating cherries is good for self-esteem, confidence, and general well-being.

Cypress

The cypress symbolized fertility and rebirth to the ancient Phoenicians and was sacred to the goddess Ashtart. The ancient Greeks revered the cypress as being sacred to Artemis. However, as the cypress tree will not sprout again once it has been cut, it is sometimes used to symbolize the finality of death.

In the Christian tradition, the cypress represents stoicism, patience, and standing up for what is true. Consequently, it is sometimes known as "the Christian tree." The cypress tree is found in many graveyards around the Mediterranean Sea, as it is an evergreen tree that symbolizes the resurrection.

Elder

Although the elder tree is a rather unattractive shrub or small tree with unpleasant-smelling flowers, it has been used for magical and medicinal purposes since Egyptian times. Virtually every part of the elder can be used medicinally. The inner bark makes an effective emetic; the leaves can relieve sprains, bruises and headaches; and a tea made from the blossoms helps relieve inflamed sinuses. The berries also stimulate the immune system.

The Golden Legend, by Jacobus de Voragine (c. 1230–1298), was a famous book in medieval times. The common beliefs that the cross of Christ was made from elder and that Judas Iscariot hanged himself from an elder tree come from this book. In fact, both are unlikely, as it is doubtful that elder was growing in Palestine at that time.

Throughout Europe the elder tree has been considered a guardian tree that protects the household. Until the nineteenth century people regularly placed offerings of food and drink in front of their guardian elders.

In parts of Europe, a cross of elder was placed on graves after a funeral. If it flowered, it was a certain sign that the soul of the departed one had reached heaven.

The Druids carried an elder branch in Beltane rituals to honor the crone. The berries of the elder are gathered on St. John's Eve and used as charms to protect people from witchcraft. A wand made from an elder branch wards off any form of psychic attack.

Fig

The fig tree was held in veneration everywhere it grew, as it symbolized the male and female principles. Its three-lobed leaf represents the male genitalia, and its fruit, the female. Because the fruit appears similar to female breasts, eating the fruit was thought to help women become pregnant. The fig is sometimes known as the "many-breasted tree." Because of all this, the fig was sometimes used as an aphrodisiac. Some people believe the Tree of Knowledge in the Garden of Eden is a fig tree. As Mohammed swore an oath on it, the fig tree is a sacred tree in Islam. In the Hebrew tradition, the fig tree symbolizes peace and prosperity. The fig tree is the first plant to be mentioned by name in the Bible: "[Adam and Eve] knew that they were naked; and they sewed fig leaves together, and made themselves aprons." (Genesis 3:7) The fig tree is mentioned thirty-seven times in the Old Testament.

Romulus and Remus were said to have sheltered under a fig tree where they were suckled by a wolf. A famous fig tree, known as the "Ruminal Fig," stood on the Palatine Hill on the spot where the Tiber river was believed to have washed the two babies ashore. The Romans considered the fig and the fig tree to be symbols of good luck.[5]

Even today, the fig is an ingredient in love potions. Women sometimes use gifts of figs to attract and charm men.

See also *Banyan*.

---

5. Fred Hageneder, *The Meaning of Trees* (San Francisco: Chronicle Books, 2005), 93.

Fir

The fir tree symbolizes honesty. In Chinese symbology it is related to patience.

As a Christmas tree, the fir symbolizes the winter solstice, the birth of Jesus, and the start of a new year. It is the tree of rebirth and immortality. The charming tradition of decorating a fir tree at Christmas dates back to sixteenth-century Germany, when Christmas trees were decorated with apples, candles, and colored paper. This tradition spread to Britain and the United States in the nineteenth century. Yet the use of a fir tree to celebrate the death of the old year and the birth of the new actually dates back to Roman times, when evergreen trees were used at the feast of Saturnalia.

Hawthorn

In ancient Greece, brides wore crowns of hawthorn. This is because the hawthorn was sacred to Artemis and Hymen, the god of marriage. The Greeks also chewed hawthorn leaves at funerals and purification ceremonies because they symbolized hope. The Romans made a tea from the leaves to repel the spells of witches. Leaves were also strewn in cradles to protect babies from the attacks of witches.[6]

Hawthorn and yew trees are considered attractive to fairies. Because of this, it is extremely unlucky to harm them in any way.

It is also considered unlucky to bring hawthorn inside the home. However, outdoors the hawthorn signifies cleansing and purification.

In Turkey, men considered the hawthorn blossom to be highly erotic, and related its scent to female sexuality.

The famous Glastonbury thorn is reputed to have grown from the staff of Joseph of Arimathea, who plunged it into the ground when he arrived in Britain in 63 CE. Puritans destroyed the origi-

---

6. Alice Thoms Vitale, *Leaves in Myth, Magic and Medicine* (New York: Stewart, Tabori and Chang, 1997), 150.

nal tree in 1643, and the thorn that grows there today comes from a cutting taken from it.

Hazel

Magic wands are mentioned in ancient Chaldean and Egyptian records. Hazel has been one of the main sources of wood for magic wands for thousands of years. Apollo gave Mercury a hazel wand, which he used to instill good virtues into humankind. In Scandinavia, the hazel was sacred to Thor and was used as a protection against lightning. In Hebrew tradition, Adam took a hazel branch with him from the Garden of Eden. Noah carried it in his ark and after that it passed through several hands—including Abraham, Isaac, and Jacob—before becoming the rod of Moses. In Irish tradition, St. Patrick used a hazel rod to banish all the snakes from Ireland.

Pliny (23–79 CE) wrote about the use of hazel rods in water divining. They are still used for this purpose today. Traditionally, divining rods were cut from the eastern side of the tree at auspicious times—usually at night, either on a holy day or the start of the new moon. The person preparing the rod had to face east, and afterward the freshly cut rod had to be presented to the rising sun.

The Celts considered the hazel a tree of wisdom, and people could increase their knowledge by eating hazelnuts. An old saying has it that all your wishes will come true if you carry a twig of hazel as an amulet or charm.

Holly

Holly was sacred to the Druids. In northern Europe, holly is brought indoors at Christmastime as it symbolizes life and, in the middle of winter, the promise of new life. The Japanese hang holly outside their homes at New Year to ward off evil spirits.

Medieval Christians associated Jesus with holly, possibly because the derivation of the word *holly* comes from the Anglo-Saxon *holegn*, which means "holy." Consequently, it was used to decorate churches at Christmastime.

A number of superstitions gradually became connected with holly. In England, it was considered bad luck to bring holly into the house before Christmas day, and it had to be taken down on Twelfth Night. Single women were advised to attach a sprig of holly to their bedpost. Doing so prevented them from becoming witches. Today, the custom of decorating homes with holly at Christmastime is still practiced. In fact, the demand for holly is so great that commercial holly farms have been established to cater to this need.

Keeping holly berries in your pocket is believed to provide protection and ward off negative energies.

Mistletoe

Mistletoe was sacred to the Druids, who believed it possessed powerful healing qualities. In fact, in folk medicine, mistletoe is frequently called "allheal." It is a parasite that lives on oak trees. The evergreen mistletoe, with no roots in the ground, must have fascinated the Druids, especially in winter when they thought the host tree was dead. The Druids revered the oak tree, and to find mistletoe growing on an oak was extremely propitious. Bunches of mistletoe can be hung around the house at the time of the winter solstice to provide protection for the inhabitants.

Kissing under mistletoe is a happy tradition with two possible origins. One says the Celts used it as a symbol of peace. Enemies who met in the forest beneath the mistletoe would kiss each other and be friends for at least that one day. Another possibility comes from Norse mythology. Balder, god of the summer sun, was killed by an arrow that had been poisoned with mistletoe. His mother's tears of grief created the white berries that are found on mistletoe. When Balder was resurrected, his mother was so happy that she hung up mistletoe and kissed everyone who passed beneath it.

Because of its strong association with the Druids, the early Christian church refused to allow mistletoe to be used for church decoration.

Oak

In ancient Greece and Rome, oak trees symbolized strength, power, and endurance. They were sacred to Artemis, Cybele, Hecate, and Zeus. Dodona, a healing and oracle center in Greece, was situated in an oak forest, and the priests and priestesses listened to the sounds created by the ancient trees, amplified by bronze vessels that vibrated in the wind.

The Romans celebrated the marriage of Jupiter and Juno every year. As they were the god and goddess of the oak, the ceremony was always held in a sacred grove of oak trees. The Romans crowned their heroes with a wreath of oak leaves. As a result, the oak became a symbol of steadfastness and courage.

The Hebrews associated the oak tree with pagan worship. However, in the Bible the angel of the Lord appeared to Gideon while he was sitting under an oak tree (Judges 6:11–21). The famous Oak of Moreh in Israel was known as the "oak of the soothsayer" or the "oak which giveth oracles."

At the time of the Druids, the oak was the most sacred tree in Europe. The death penalty applied to anyone who damaged an oak tree.

In Scandinavia, the oak tree was sacred to Thor and was known as the "thunder tree." At one time people kept oak branches in their homes to protect themselves from lightning.

In Japan, oak trees represented protection and good luck. Even today during the Japanese New Year, many people place oak branches at their front gates to attract the gods and good luck for the coming year.

The Native Americans dedicated the oak tree to Mother Earth.

Oak trees provided protection from evil spirits. They also provided luck, and newly married couples used to dance around an oak tree to gain good fortune and a happy marriage.

Another belief that is still often practiced today is to stand under an oak tree in autumn and try to catch a leaf before it touches the ground. Keep this leaf in your purse or wallet. Doing so ensures you will never run out of money. It is also considered extremely fortunate for an oak leaf to accidentally land on you. This leaf should be kept in a safe place and will provide you with good luck.

Walt Whitman (1819–1892) understood the magic of nature very well. I've always loved the phrase "joyous leaves," which he uses three times in his poem "I Saw in Louisiana a Live-Oak Growing," published in his anthology *Leaves of Grass* (1855):

> I saw in Louisiana a live-oak growing,
> All alone stood it,
> and the moss hung down from the branches,
> Without any companion it stood there
> uttering joyous leaves of dark green.

The acorn has always been considered a symbol of wisdom and prosperity. An old folk belief says you can protect yourself from evil and the vagaries of the weather by keeping an acorn in your pocket. If you carry three acorns in your pocket you will always look younger than your years.

Pine

The pine was an important tree to the ancient Greeks and was sacred to Aphrodite, Dionysus, and Pan. Because it is an evergreen, the pine became associated with birth, life, and immortality. In Phoenician mythology, Attis, the sun god, died under a pine tree, and was born again in the spring. The pinecone was considered an emblem of fertility, good health, and good luck. In Japan, the cedar, chestnut, and pine are believed to be the earthly homes of gods.

Because it can grow in the harshest of conditions, the pine is considered by the Chinese to be a symbol of longevity and winter.

Poplar

The poplar has always been considered a magical tree because its leaves tremble. It is believed to cure agues and fevers. In Lincolnshire, a popular charm involved someone who was ill cutting off a lock of their hair and tying it around a branch of a poplar while reciting:

> When Christ Our Lord was on the Cross,
> Then didst thou sadly shiver and toss.
> My aches and pains thou now must take,
> Instead of me I bid thee shake.[7]

Another belief says your wealth will increase if you carry a small piece of poplar everywhere you go.

Rowan

Rowan, or mountain ash, is most abundant in northern Europe and has always been used as a protection against witchcraft. If a branch of rowan touched a witch, she would immediately be taken away by the devil.

Rowan is frequently found close to ancient stone circles. For that reason, it is possible the ancient Druids considered it a sacred tree.

Rowan trees were planted close to homes to protect them from lightning and to bring good luck to the household. They were also planted in cemeteries to protect people from ghosts. Boats made from rowan were believed to gain protection from the wood.

---

7. E. Radford and M. A. Radford, edited and revised by Christina Hole, *Encyclopaedia of Superstitions* (London: Hutchinson and Company, 1961), 270. Originally published in 1948.

Rowan is mentioned early in Scandinavian mythology. Because it helped Thor cross a treacherous and dangerous river, it was called "Thor's helper."

Crosses made of rowan twigs were used to protect farm animals. They were also used to protect babies before they were baptized. Not much more than a hundred years ago, crosses made from rowan and birch were hung over the front door of every cottage. They were also used to protect pigsties and seedbeds.[8] The berries from the rowan can be worn as a necklace to ward off the evil eye.

Sycamore

The ancient Egyptians believed two sycamore trees protected the entrance of heaven. This was in the east where Ra, the sun god, rose every morning. The goddess Nuit, who was sacred to the sycamore, gave food and water to the dead souls on their way to the next world. Once they'd accepted her offering, they could never turn back.

The long-living sycamore symbolizes growth, expansion, persistence, and strength. It is sometimes used in healing potions and spells involving regeneration.

Thorn

There are several varieties of thorn. The Roman soldiers put a crown of thorns on the head of Jesus before His crucifixion. Medieval Christians thought this crown was made from blackthorn, but it is more likely to have come from a spiny shrub known today as Christ thorn (*Ziziphus spina-christi*). God appeared to Moses in a burning bush (Exodus 3:2). In Hebrew tradition, this was *Acacia nilotica*, a thorn bush. In British tradition, Joseph of Arimathea's staff turned into a thorn bush when he struck it into the ground at Glastonbury (see *Hawthorn*). This thorn flowers at Christmastime to celebrate the birth of Christ.

---

8. *Encyclopedia of Magic and Superstition* (London: Octopus Books, 1974), 217.

At one time, blackthorn was associated with witches who used it in various magical rituals. Even Satan was believed to use a spine of blackthorn to prick the mark of the devil on his supporters.

Yew

Yew trees are extremely old and have been growing since before the ice ages. Because it has survived for so long, the yew is considered a tree of longevity, everlasting life, and rebirth. The yew is a slow-growing tree that can live up to three thousand years. It is considered the most powerful tree of all for providing protection from evil forces. The Druids believed the yew symbolized the path from life to death. The ancient Greeks considered the yew a portal to the Underworld.

• • •

In the next chapter we will look at tree magic.

two

Tree Magic

*W*ithout exception, every human being benefits from spending time outdoors connecting with nature. Not everyone is able to walk in the countryside, but all of us have access to parks or gardens. Slow down and enjoy the beauty of nature in all its moods. Sit quietly and meditate or relax. Try talking to some of the trees around you. You don't have to do this out loud if you don't want to, or if you happen to be somewhere where it may not be appropriate. Listen carefully to hear what the trees say to you. You might have to use your imagination at first, but in time you'll be able to enjoy mutually beneficial conversations with plant life wherever you go.

Trees have been used for magical purposes for thousands of years, and many people still use them today. Whenever possible, I prefer to perform my rituals outdoors, and I usually perform them close to my oracle tree.

Oracle tree

An oracle tree is an ancient Celtic idea. They believed trees connected heaven and Earth. For this reason, oracle trees could be used to mediate between humans and the gods. The easiest way to find your own personal oracle tree is to hug trees that appeal to you. The tree that is destined to be your oracle tree will respond to your hug in a different way from other trees. You may need to hug dozens of trees before you find the right one. Do not hug every tree you come across. Choose trees that are aesthetically pleasing to you. I prefer to find my oracle trees in reasonably remote locations where I am not likely to be disturbed.

Once you find your oracle tree you will enter into a symbiotic relationship with it. The tree is likely to ask you to become the guardian of the area around it. This means you need to tend to the needs of everything in the vicinity of your oracle tree. In return, the oracle tree will provide you with protection, love, and insight.

Visit your oracle tree as often as possible. Hug it, sit beside it, ask it questions, listen expectantly for what it has to say, look after the area it is situated in, and enjoy its company.

The area around your oracle tree will quickly become a sacred space for you, a place where you become aware of your own spirituality and can make contact with the Divine. The spirit of your sacred space will communicate with your inner spirit. Because you have made a commitment to look after the area, you will receive unexpected help from nature spirits and from the universe itself. Accept this help, and work with it.

You will derive enormous benefits from doing so. In return, you can send out love and healing to individuals, places, and the whole planet. You may find it helpful to do this as a ritual, visualizing yourself surrounded by a pure white light of love, which you send out to every corner of the world.

Your oracle tree will also heal you whenever necessary. If you feel downhearted, upset, or depressed, talk to your oracle tree. Sit with your back leaning against its trunk and allow its healing energies to restore and revitalize you. I know from personal experience that this also works extremely well for headaches. Your oracle tree will help you with more serious health problems, too. Sit under the tree, with your back against its trunk, and talk openly to the tree about your concerns. Ask for love and healing. Repeat this as often as possible until your health has been restored.

Releasing Negativity

We all have negative thoughts from time to time. Most of the time these are not a problem as they are outnumbered by our positive thoughts. However, negative thoughts can become a threat to our health and well-being if we find ourselves constantly dwelling on them. Fortunately, trees are willing to absorb our negative thoughts and transmute them into energies they can use.

Although I could do so, I do not use my oracle tree for this purpose. This is simply personal preference. I use a different tree every time I wish to release any negativity.

Walk through a park or any other place that has a variety of trees to choose from. Stand somewhere where you are surrounded by trees and close your eyes for a few seconds. Take three slow, deep breaths and think of your need to find a tree that is willing to release your negativity. Open your eyes again and start walking. Your intuition will lead you to the tree that is perfect for you at that moment.

Stop walking when you feel you have found the right tree. Mentally ask the tree if you can touch it. If you receive a positive response, thank the tree and place a hand on it. If you receive no response at all, mentally thank the tree for listening and start walking again until you find another tree. Continue doing this until you find a tree that responds positively. In practice, I have never received more than one rejection before receiving a positive response. I believe all trees wish us well, and the only time we ever get a negative response is when a tree knows that another tree nearby will be more suitable for our needs.

Spend a few minutes silently communicating with the tree. You might stroke it or give it a hug while enjoying an intuitive conversation. When the time seems right, ask the tree if you can give it all the negativity that you have unintentionally gathered in your body. If you have made friends with the tree, you will always receive a positive response.

Stand as close to the tree as you can with your back against it. Place your hands behind you so they can touch the tree, too. Close your eyes and thank the tree for releasing all of the negativity from your body. You will notice a number of changes in your body as you do this exercise. You may feel as if the negativity is being pulled out of you. You may feel a positive response in one or more of your chakras. Stay in this position until you feel all of the negativity has been released. Turn around and give the tree a hug, thanking it for helping you.

A friend of mine releases his negativity in a different way. Once he's found the right tree and gained permission to give it his negativity, he rubs his hands vigorously over his body to collect the negativity in his hands. He then releases it by rubbing his hands on the trunk of the tree. He does this several times until he feels all the negativity has gone.

Experiment with both of these methods and see which one works better for you. Try other methods, too. Your intuition might tell you to do something completely different. If so, that may well be the best method for you.

The Gentle Art of Tree Hugging

I have always enjoyed hugging trees, and I have gained considerable benefit from it. Tree hugging could be considered a form of meditation, and it is useful on those grounds alone. However, I find it much more than that. It puts me in touch with the soul of the tree, allowing me to receive information I could never learn in any other way. After hugging a tree, my mind is at peace and my energy is revitalized. Old trees, in particular, are wonderful sources of energy. This energy can be obtained in three ways: by touching a tree, by sitting with your back against the trunk, or by hugging a tree.

Almost everyone has heard of tree hugging. Unfortunately, people who do not know any better sometimes use the term in an attempt to belittle people who enjoy hugging trees. At one time I tried to convince these people to experiment with tree hugging, but found it a waste of time. People need to discover the benefits of tree hugging in their own way.

Consequently, if you have not hugged trees before, experiment somewhere where you are unlikely to be disturbed. Practice either on your own or with someone who is open-minded about the subject.

There is no right or wrong way to hug a tree. Any contact is good. However, the most effective way I have found to hug a tree is to have my heart and brow chakras in contact with the trunk of the tree. This is how to do it:

1. Select a suitable tree. I choose trees that appear to be good, healthy examples of their species. I prefer older trees with thick trunks. Look for trees that are aesthetically pleasing to you. In many cases, the tree will seem to choose you rather than the other way around. You may need to hug several trees before finding one that "feels" right for you.

2. Stand facing the tree with your legs apart. Smile at the tree for a few seconds and then lean into it to allow your chest, home to the heart chakra, to make contact with the tree trunk. Place your arms around the trunk in a gentle caress. Rest your forehead against the trunk. Take a slow, deep breath and close your eyes.

3. Continue breathing slowly using your diaphragm. Allow as much time as necessary to really feel the sensation of your chest touching the tree. You will gradually notice a sense of comfort, peace, and tranquility.

4. Enjoy this sensation for about half a minute and then focus your attention on your forehead, home of your brow chakra and third eye.

5. Gently alternate your attention between the two chakras, spending approximately thirty seconds on each one before changing focus.

6. Allow yourself to feel the energy of the tree in your hands and arms, and in any other parts of your body that are in contact with the tree. Gratefully receive the strength and power the tree is giving you.

7. Talk to the tree if you wish. You can do this mentally or out loud. Be patient and wait for a reply, which will come as a

thought in your mind. You can ask the tree questions about anything, and the conversation can last as long as you wish.

8. Continue hugging the tree while you are doing this. When you feel ready to let go, silently thank the tree first.

9. Stand in front of the tree and gently stroke it or pat it good-bye. Smile at the tree and silently express your thanks. I usually wave goodbye to it as well. Say goodbye for the last time, and carry on with your day.

On many occasions, I've been asked why I involve the chakras in this exercise. Surely, I'm told, all that is necessary is to hug the tree. Of course, many people hug trees without thinking of their chakras, but most of the time at least one chakra is involved. We'll discuss the chakras in detail in chapter 7.

When I hug a tree, I am using my heart and brow chakras. This is deliberate. My heart chakra represents universal love and understanding. The tree helps me balance this chakra so I can express my feelings effortlessly. At the same time, my brow chakra is being energized, which gives me easy access to my logical mind and psychic perceptions.

If I feel the need to balance or recharge any other chakra, I can hug the tree in a way that allows the chakra and the tree trunk to be in contact.

Some people like to energize all of their chakras by hugging the tree with their back against its trunk and their arms hugging the tree behind them. I do this sometimes, but I prefer to energize all my chakras by facing the tree while hugging it.

Tree Meditation

It may not be possible to visit your oracle tree in all weather. If it is sited a long way from your home, you may not be able to visit it regularly. You might live in the middle of a large city where it is impossible to find a suitable tree. Fortunately, you can visualize your oracle tree, or any other tree, whenever you wish.

Sit down comfortably, close your eyes, and consciously relax all the muscles in your body. Once you have done this, mentally scan your body to make sure that you are completely relaxed. If necessary, focus on any areas that are not fully relaxed and then scan again.

When you feel ready, visualize yourself in a beautiful room. You are sitting in an incredibly comfortable chair. On the wall to your right is a large picture showing a beautiful meadow with a forest in the background. The picture seems so restful and peaceful that you decide to get up and look at it more closely.

The picture is even more beautiful close up. You move closer and closer, and suddenly find yourself inside the painting, standing in the meadow. It seems perfectly natural to be inside the painting, and you look around with interest. You can smell the fresh grass and hear the birds in the trees ahead.

It is a beautiful day and you enjoy looking at the clear blue sky overhead, with just a few fluffy clouds way up high. You may see a squirrel or two darting up the trunks of the trees. A slight breeze rustles the branches of the trees, which seem to be calling to you. It is a comforting sound, and you feel safe and happy as you walk through the meadow and into this beautiful forest.

It is pleasantly cool in the forest. You take your time and walk deeper into the forest, enjoying the peace and quiet of nature. Every now and again, you pause to admire different trees. You find that you can communicate with them telepathically, and you enjoy talking with them. Some of the trees are young saplings, while others are extremely old. You discover every tree has its own distinct personality. Some are full of enthusiasm and want to talk, while others are content with a mere acknowledgment.

You find yourself walking down a beautiful glade. At the end is a magnificent tree, and you realize this is the tree you have come to see. You start walking faster, as you have so much to discuss with this tree. Soon you find yourself under it, and you give it a welcoming hug. You absorb the tree's energy and you thank it for being there for you.

You sit down under the tree with your back leaning against it. You ask it if it is willing to have a conversation with you. Once the tree has given its assent, you tell it everything that is going on in your life—all your hopes, dreams, plans, goals, concerns, and fears. You can also discuss your concerns about people close to you.

Allow the tree sufficient time to answer. You may "hear" the tree as it speaks to you. The answers are more likely to appear in your mind. Ask for further clarification, if necessary.

Once the tree has answered all your questions, ask what you can do for it. The tree might request that you spend more time caring for the natural world around your home. It might even suggest you join an ecological society, or read more about the subject.

Spend as much time communing with the tree as you wish. There is no need to rush away as soon as your questions have been answered. Enjoy the healing and spiritual energy the tree provides for as long as you wish.

When you feel it is time to go, stand up, give the tree another hug, and thank it for helping you. Walk back down the grove and through the forest. Cross the meadow and climb through the picture frame.

Allow a minute or two to become familiar with your surroundings. When you feel ready, take three slow deep breaths and open your eyes.

You'll feel refreshed and energized after this tree meditation. You'll also have gained many useful insights that will enhance your life. I find when I do this meditation that the tree at the end of the grove sometimes changes. It is usually my oracle tree, but at other times it might be a tall pine tree, an ancient oak, a weeping willow, or some other tree. I no longer worry about this, as I invariably speak to the tree I'm meant to be communicating with at the time. However, if I specifically want to speak to my oracle tree, I will request it before starting the meditation.

The Celtic Tree Alphabet

The ancient Celts loved, cherished, and revered the natural world. They considered it not as a resource to be exploited but as a nurturing presence that assists all humanity. In other words, they believed in the concept of Mother Earth.

The Druids conducted many of their ceremonies outdoors in sacred groves known as *nemetons*. The sacred trees in these groves were usually oaks. Roman writers commented on the care the Druids took in harvesting mistletoe and sacred herbs. Holy wells gave Druids an opportunity to express their love for the life-giving waters of Mother Earth.

The Celts had an interesting bardic alphabet called Ogham. This alphabet is attributed to Ogma, son of King Elathan, who devised it about 600 BCE to prove his ingenuity.[9] However, the oldest existing examples of inscriptions in Ogham date back only to the fourth century CE.

The Ogham alphabet consists of twenty-five letters, or oghams. Ogma devised twenty of these, and the other five were a later addition. The oghams were not simply an alphabet. They created a mnemonic system that encompassed the entire cosmological worldview of the Celts. Each ogham relates to a tree, color, animal, and tree month. I find that the keywords for each ogham provide fascinating insights into the nature of each tree.

Beithe: birch, white, cow, December 24–January 20. Keyword: beginnings.

Luis: rowan, red and gray, unicorn and bear, January 21–February 17. Keyword: insight.

---

9. Anonymous, *The Book of Ballymote*. This is a fourteenth-century Irish manuscript in the library of the Royal Irish Academy in Dublin. It is thought to have been copied from ninth-century texts. This manuscript says: "Ogma, being a man much skilled in dialects and poetry, invented Ogham, its object being for signs of secret speech known only to the learned, and designed to be kept from the vulgar and poor of the nation."

Fearn: alder, crimson, red fox, ram and stallion, February 18– March 17. Keyword: strength.

Saille: willow, fiery red, hare and cat, March 18–April 14. Keyword: intuition.

Nion: ash, clear green, snake, April 15–May 12. Keyword: peace.

Huath: hawthorn, purple, goat and dragon, May 13–June 9. Keyword: restraint.

Duir: oak, dark brown and black, white horse, lion and salamander, June 10–July 7. Keyword: protection.

Tinne: holly, dark gray, warhorse, July 8–August 4. Keyword: balance.

Coll: hazel, brown, salmon, August 5–September 1. Keyword: intuition.

Quert: apple, green, unicorn, September 2–29. Keyword: beauty.

Muin: vine, variegated, lizard, September 30–October 27. Keyword: prophecy.

Gort: ivy, sky blue, boar, October 28–November 24. Keyword: progress.

Ngetal: reed, grass green, dog, stag and rat, November 25– December 23. Keyword: unity.

Straif: blackthorn, bright purple, wolf, toad and black cat. Keyword: fate.

Ruis: elder, blood red, badger. Keyword: change.

Ailm: fir, pale blue, red cow. Keyword: power.

Ohn: gorse, yellow and gold, rabbit. Keyword: wisdom.

Ur: heather, purple, bee and lion. Keyword: magnificent obsession.

Eadha: aspen, silver and red, white mare. Keyword: endurance.

Ioho: yew, dark green, spider. Keyword: immortality.

In 1948, Robert Graves (1895–1985), the English poet and novelist, wrote a hugely influential book on the Celtic tradition called *The*

White Goddess.[10] His book introduced the thirteen-month tree calendar to the world, and ever since then it has played a major role in modern-day Paganism. This version of the tree calendar lists the months as:

Beithe (birch): December 24–January 20
Luis (rowan): January 21–February 17
Nion (ash): February 18–March 17
Fearn (alder): March 18–April 14
Saille (willow): April 15–May 12
Huath (hawthorn): May 13–June 9
Duir (oak): June 10–July 7
Tinne (holly): July 8–August 4
Coll (hazel): August 5–September 1
Muin (grapevine): September 2–September 29
Gort (ivy): September 30–October 27
Ngetal (reed): October 28–November 24
Ruis (elder): November 25–December 22
Mistletoe: December 23 (Midwinter Day)

Commercially made oracle cards and ogham sticks are available if you are interested in learning about the divination aspects of Ogham.[11]

---

10. Robert Graves, *The White Goddess: A Historical Grammar of Poetic Myth* (New York: Farrar, Strauss and Cudahy, 1948).

11. Richard Webster, *Omens, Oghams and Oracles: Divination in the Druidic Tradition* (St. Paul, MN: Llewellyn, 1995). This book explains several Druidic methods of divination, including the oghams. Matthew Flesch, *Ogham: Druidic Oracle of the Trees* (Dragon Torque Press, 1997). This is a set of ogham sticks and a 72-page book of instructions. Liz Murray and Colin Murray, *The Celtic Tree Oracle: A System of Divination* (New York: St. Martin's Press, 1988).

three

The World of Flowers

lowers can be beautiful, delicate, colorful, and scented. It is not surprising that early people were attracted to them just as much as we are today. Because they have such a short life span, flowers were associated not only with youth, beauty, and love, but also with the transitory nature of life itself.

Long before flower gardens were invented, people used flowers as perfumes, medicines, and food. They were also strewn on graves and used as offerings to the gods. Consequently, flowers have always had magical connotations.

The ancient Greeks had a floral goddess named Chloris. The Romans called her Flora and held an annual celebration for her each year called Floralia. Many depictions of her survive, especially on coins. She is usually shown either holding flowers or scattering flower petals.

The custom of strewing flowers on graves was common in the Greco-Roman period, but it had been practiced for centuries before that. The early Christians did not approve of this custom but were forced to accept it, as it had become so popular.

In the seventeenth century, flowers and herbs were strewn along the path the bride and groom took from their homes to the church. William Browne (1591–1643) described a Devonshire village wedding in his *Britannia's Pastorals* (1613):

> As I haue seene vpon a Bridall day
> Full many maids clad in their best array,
> In honour of the Bride come with their flaskets
> Fill'd with flowers: others in wicker baskets
> Bring from the marish rushes, to o'er-spread
> The ground, whereon to church the louers tread:
> Whilst that the quaintest youth of all the plaine
> Vshers their way with many a piping straine.

In medieval Europe, plants were used for many purposes. Parsley, for instance, was believed to prevent drunkenness. Anise could eliminate nightmares, and laurel encouraged prophetic dreams.

Fortunetellers were able to predict the fate of people who were ill by placing a sprig of vervain on the sick person's head. People who had been robbed could place heliotrope under their pillows and be confident of having a dream that would reveal the identity of the thief.

In Victorian times, flowers were considered so important that many floral gardens were planted—not with the intention of creating beauty but to provide the raw materials for cooking, medicines, perfumes, and a variety of handcrafts.

A gift of flowers brings happiness and good luck to both the giver and the recipient.

Flowers as Symbols

Individual flowers have their own symbolic meanings. Flowers, in general, symbolize femininity, innocence, manifestation, love, and the soul.

Flowers also symbolize spiritual awakening in many religions. Both Brahma and Buddha are frequently depicted emerging from flowers. The Virgin Mary often holds an iris or a lily. The lily is associated with repentance, and is said to have grown from the tears Eve shed when she was banished from the Garden of Eden. Flowers can also symbolize death and rebirth. This is why the Romans scattered roses on their graves. The Taoists use a golden blossom flowering from a person's head to symbolize wisdom.

Ikebana, the Japanese art of flower arranging, has its own complex symbology that reflects the ideals of Zen Buddhism. The flowers are arranged in a triad that symbolizes heaven, mankind, and Earth. As these three elements symbolize a perfect universe, the sprays of flowers must also be arranged in a perfect, apparently effortless manner. An alternative arrangement ensures all the plants point downward in a flowing manner to illustrate the gradual decline of life. Conversely, another school, known as *rikka*, or "standing" school, places all the flowers in an upright position to symbolize fidelity to God, the Emperor, or a life partner. Rikka arrangements are deliberately asymmetrical, as they symbolize an aspect of nature that is never perfect.

In the 1960s, the flower children adopted the flower as a symbol of peace.

Flowers and Superstition

There are numerous superstitions about flowers. It has, for instance, always been considered a bad omen for a flower to bloom out of season. Certain flowers should not be brought indoors as they will cause a death to occur in the family. Dreaming of white flowers is another sign of a death in the family. It is bad luck to pick up cut flowers that you happen to see lying on the ground when you are out and about. They cause bad luck and possibly even death.

Actors do not like live flowers on stage as they consider them unlucky. They prefer using artificial flowers to decorate the stage. The exception to this is the bouquet presented to performers at the end of the performance.

Flowers in the Christian Tradition

A charming story explains that the aspen trembles because the cross of Jesus was made from its wood. Another legend says that the cross was made from the elder, and Judas Iscariot was supposed to have hanged himself from an elder tree. As a result of this, the oval fungal excrescences that appear on its bark are sometimes called "Judas' ears." William Shakespeare wrote in *Love's Labour's Lost* (act 5, scene 11) that Judas was hanged from an elder tree. Yet another tradition says that Judas hanged himself from a fig tree.

The passionflower is a plant of the genus Passiflora. Sixteenth-century Spanish missionaries probably named it thus because of its numerous associations with the Passion of Christ. The leaf of the plant symbolizes the spear. The five petals and five sepals represent ten Apostles—only ten because Peter and Judas Iscariot were not included, Peter because he denied Christ and Judas Iscariot because he betrayed Christ. The five anthers represent the five wounds; the tendrils symbolize the scourges; the column of the ovary depicts the pillar of the cross; the stamens represent the hammers; the three stigmas, the three nails; the filaments within the flower symbolize the crown of thorns; and the calyx represents the nimbus or glory. Finally, the white tint of the flower symbolizes purity and the blue tint, heaven. This plant also stays open for three days, which symbolizes the three days from the crucifixion to the resurrection.

Adam and Eve used a fig leaf to cover their nakedness after eating the forbidden fruit.

A number of flowers are said to have received spots of Christ's blood when he was on the cross. These plants still have stained blossoms today: red anemone, the arum, the purple orchis, and the spotted persicaria. The vervain is often included as it has leaves that are spotted with crimson.

A number of plants have also been dedicated to Christian saints. These include:

Crocus—St. Valentine
Daisy—St. Margaret
Lady's smock—the Virgin Mary
Rose—Mary Magdalene
St. John's wort—St. John

Flowers as Food

Our forbears knew which foods were edible and which were poisonous. Many poisonous plants could be determined by their bitter taste and were left alone, while their edible cousins were picked and eaten.

Seeds were a common part of people's diets, as shown by the seeds found in the stomach of the Tollund Man, who experienced a violent death some 2,400 years ago. His body was preserved in a peat bog in Denmark until it was rediscovered in 1950. His last meal had been a soup containing vegetables and seeds: barley, gold of pleasure (*Camelina sativa*), linseed, knotweed, bristlegrass, and chamomile. Some of the seeds were hard to find and had been collected and stored, presumably for a special occasion. Seeds are particularly useful as they are rich in protein and also contain carbohydrates.

Roots were also extremely useful, and a wide variety of them were eaten until the potato was introduced to Europe in about 1570. Even then, it took until the 1780s before the potato became popular.

Many flowers are still consumed today, usually as culinary herbs. Several members of the mint family are used as flavorings and also to help cure coughs and jaundice.

Throughout history many flowers have been used for healing and magical purposes. Here are some of the most important ones:

Anemone

According to Greco-Roman mythology, the red anemone was created from the blood of Adonis as he lay dying. He had been hunting and was gored by a wild boar. Anemones grew where his blood and the tears of the grieving goddess of love, Aphrodite, fell on the ground. As a result, the anemone is associated with beauty, love, and youthful energy and enthusiasm. The Christian church also related the red of the anemone with the blood shed by Jesus at his crucifixion.

According to folklore, menstruation can be induced by drinking water that has been boiled with anemone leaves.

Angelica

Angelica leaves can be carried, worn, or placed around the house to deter evil spirits.

Carnation

The carnation is an important flower in the Christian tradition, as it is believed carnations sprang up everywhere the Virgin Mary's tears fell as she walked to her son's crucifixion. In Mexico, carnations are known as "the flowers of the dead." They are strewn around the bodies of dead people who are being prepared for their burials. In the Netherlands, the red carnation was associated with love.

Carnations remove negative energy, especially problems in close relationships. Red carnations, in particular, also provide energy and optimism.

Chicory

Chicory has always had a magical reputation, and at one time people believed that anyone who held it became invisible. People also believed that if chicory was picked at noon with a gold knife and held against a lock, the lock would open.

Chrysanthemum

The chrysanthemum is a universal symbol of autumn. In the West, artists have used it to symbolize death and decay. In the East, the chrysanthemum symbolizes good luck, happiness, longevity, and wealth. The chrysanthemum is one of the five beneficial flowers in feng shui, and represents happiness and laughter. In Japan, the chrysanthemum is on the official seal of the imperial family. This is because its radiating petals look like the rays of the sun.

Tea made from chrysanthemum is used for its cooling properties and is especially useful for people with fevers.

Cowslip

Cowslips are sometimes called *Herb Peter* after St. Peter, who holds the keys to heaven. This is because the flowers remind people of a bunch of keys.

In the seventeenth century, housewives made preserves and drinks from cowslip flowers to cure memory loss, insomnia, and nervousness. Even today, some people make a tea and jelly from these wildflowers to ensure a good night's sleep.

Cyclamen

Because the leaves of the cyclamen resemble the human ear, this plant was considered a useful medicine for any problems with hearing or the ear itself. In the Middle Ages, men who were concerned about losing their hair stuffed their noses with cyclamen to prevent losing any more.

Cyclamen has long been associated with love and romance, and has been used to create love charms and aphrodisiacs. The root of the plant was commonly used to reduce the pain of childbirth. John Gerard (1545–1612), an English writer and landscape designer, wrote that cyclamen plants should be fenced in, as "any good matron might accidentally step over them bringing about a miscarriage."[12]

Daffodil

The daffodil has always been considered a cheerful flower that raises the spirits. The root of the daffodil can be squashed and applied to wounds and bruises to relieve pain and inflammation.

Daisy

Bellis, the botanical name for the daisy, is a Greek word that means "war." This name may have been applied because this plant was used to disinfect the wounds of injured soldiers. The more modern expression "lying beneath the daisies" may allude to dead soldiers buried beneath a field of daisies.

In the Christian tradition, the daisy symbolizes innocence. Consequently, it was associated with the Virgin Mary and the infant Jesus.

Medieval knights wore daisies when embarking on a quest. This told everyone they were fighting in the name of the lady they loved.

---

12. John Gerard, *Herball or Generall Historie of Plantes*. Originally published in 1597. A reprint of the revised edition (1633) was published by Lawrie and Hanley, Manchester, UK, 1882, 87.

Possibly as a result of this, daisies became a symbol of steadfastness and loyalty in love.

The tradition of a woman plucking daisy petals while reciting "He loves me, he loves me not" dates back to Victorian times. The last petal plucked reveals whether or not he actually loves her.

A paste to relieve aches and pains can be made by grinding up daisies.

Dandelion

A tea made from the roots of the dandelion can relieve chest pain. You will experience more vivid dreams if you place dried dandelion flowers under your pillow. Some people prefer to sew them into a special dream pillow. Drinking dandelion tea, especially at the full moon, increases psychic ability.

Geranium

The geranium is a positive flower that boosts confidence and self-esteem. It is also useful in helping people recover after a relationship breakup. It is better to admire geraniums outdoors, but a vase of geraniums indoors is also helpful.

Honeysuckle

Folklore says that a wedding will follow soon after you bring honeysuckle into your home. Placing a posy or vase of honeysuckle in your bedroom encourages dreams of love and romance.

Iris

The Virgin Mary is usually shown holding a lily. However, in German art she is more likely to be holding an iris. Iris was the goddess Juno's messenger, and carried messages from the gods to Earth along a rainbow-colored path that shone brilliantly after rain. Whenever a rainbow appeared, it was a sign that Iris was bringing a message. The iris is also the colorful band that surrounds the pupil of the eye. It is no wonder that Plutarch, the Greek historian, called the iris the "eye of heaven."

The iris has always had a close relationship to women, and the ancient Greeks planted irises on the graves of women to ensure Iris would guide their souls to the Elysian Fields. In Virgil's *Aeneid*, Iris took a lock of the dying queen Dido's hair to release her soul from her body.

The French have always had a strong affection for the iris, and it was the original fleur-de-lis on their heraldry. Tradition says that King Clovis (c. 465–511) was leading his army when they were blocked by a river. He noticed irises growing in the water, and realized it was shallow enough to cross. His army crossed the river and won the battle. Afterward, his soldiers picked the irises and made crowns from them.

Lily

In Greek and Roman times, the lily was associated with Venus, and symbolized chastity and purity. The early Christians borrowed this symbolism and associated the white petals and sweet fragrance of the lily with the Virgin Mary. An old legend says that lilies grew from the tears of Eve as she walked out of the Garden of Eden.

However, there has always been another, different interpretation of the lily, associating it with virility and sensuality. In ancient Egypt, it was associated with Ashtar, a goddess of fertility and creation.

Lilies are frequently seen at weddings and funerals. At weddings they symbolize innocence and purity. At funerals they represent the soul, free from the body and free from sin.

Lilies are supposed to repel ghosts and were frequently planted around houses to provide protection for the inhabitants.

In the East, the day lily (*Hemerocallis*) was believed to dispel the pangs of grief. Women wore this lily in their belts to help them forget their sorrows and grief.

Lotus

Hindus and Buddhists consider the lotus an emblem of purity, as its beautiful flower comes from a plant that grows in slime. A thousand-petaled lotus symbolizes spiritual enlightenment. The lotus has always had sexual connotations, and the two names for it in Sanskrit (*padma* and *kamala*) are also used to describe the vagina. The lotus blossom is also a symbol of the vagina in China.

The ancient Egyptians believed the goddess Isis was born from a lotus flower, and so they associated the lotus with fertility and sexual potency. The Hindus believe the creator god Brahma was born from a golden lotus flower that was sited in the navel of the universe. One legend about Buddha says that everywhere he walked, he left lotuses behind him instead of footprints.

Marigold

The marigold was associated with Apollo, the Greek god of the sun. The Greeks told a story about the Nereid Clytie who was spurned by Apollo and turned into a marigold. Ever since then, marigolds have turned to face the sun. (This same story is also told about the sunflower.) The seeds of the marigold were sometimes worn as an amulet to protect the wearer from theft. At one time it was believed adulterous women were not able to enter any church that contained marigolds.

Marigolds were frequently used in love charms and in wedding decorations. As a result, they came to symbolize faithfulness and long-lasting relationships.

Narcissus

The narcissus is named after a handsome Greek youth of that name who fell in love with his reflection in the water. He either drowned while trying to embrace his own reflection or pined away while sitting beside a pool. A flower appeared where he had sat, and the nymphs called it *narcissus*. The term *narcissist* describes someone who is cold, inward looking, and selfish. Another legend involving the narcissus tells of Persephone, who was picking narcissi in a field, when Hades, the god of the Underworld, kidnapped her and forced her to marry him.

Poppy

Opium was made from the variety of poppy commonly found around the Mediterranean. It was used to relieve pain and induce sleep. The Greeks associated it with Hypnos, the god of sleep, and Morpheus, the god of dreams. Morphine is made from opium and was named after Morpheus. In Greek mythology, Persephone was picking poppies when Hades abducted her.

Because it produces a large amount of seeds, the poppy is also associated with fertility.

Since World War I, the poppy has been adopted as the flower of remembrance in the British Commonwealth, and millions of artificial poppies are sold each year to be worn on Remembrance Day.

Primrose

It is bad luck to see a single primrose. The remedy for this is to dance around it three times while snapping your fingers. Originally, a single primrose meant that your hens would lay few eggs in the following twelve months, but gradually it became a general sign of bad luck.

However, it is extremely good luck to see thirteen or more primroses at the same time. This means you will be lucky for the next twelve months.

If you place a posy of primroses on your doorstep, according to legend, fairies will visit your home while you are asleep and bless all the inhabitants.

Rose

The rose has always symbolized beauty, love, and fertility. The rose was sacred to Aphrodite and Venus, the Greek and Roman goddesses of love. The Romans frequently planted roses on graves, as they considered the rose to be a symbol of rebirth. The Zoroastrians associated the rose with innocence, and believed its thorns appeared after evil came into the world. In Islam the rose is associated with paradise.

In the Christian tradition, the rose symbolizes the Virgin Mary's purity and beauty. The thorns symbolize her suffering at the crucifixion of her son. Red roses symbolize martyrs who have died for the Christian faith, while white roses symbolize purity of heart. One ancient Christian legend says that until Adam and Eve were expelled from the Garden of Eden roses had no thorns. God added these to remind people that they no longer lived in a perfect world.

The expression *sub rosa* ("under the rose") dates back to Roman times when roses, especially white ones, were related to Harpocrates, the god of silence. Anything said under the rose had to remain secret. In medieval times, many ceilings contained a carved or painted rose that enabled people to talk freely, knowing their words would not be repeated later.

An old belief says that all roses were originally white, but some became red after being stained with blood. There are many stories about the various people whose blood was shed. The ancient Greeks thought it was Adonis or Aphrodite. Christians believe the Crown of Thorns was made from rose-briar, and consequently it was the blood of Jesus. An old legend says red roses sprang up around the cross wherever the blood of Jesus fell. Muslims believe the blood came from Mohammed.

Rosemary

The sweet-scented rosemary symbolizes true love and remembrance. Consequently, it is seen at both marriages and funerals. In the seventeenth century, brides wore rosemary in their bridal wreaths and the bridesmaids and groom carried branches of gilded rosemary during the bridal procession. Sprigs of rosemary were also dipped into wine at the wedding reception to create a lucky charm for the couple to keep. Rosemary was sold as a protective amulet during the plague in the seventeenth century. Until early in the twentieth century, unmarried women in Britain would place a sixpence and a sprig of rosemary under their pillows on All Hallows' Eve (October 31st). Doing so ensured they would dream of their future husband.

Anne of Cleves wore a crown of rosemary when she married King Henry VIII. This may have been a fortunate choice, as she fared better than most of his other wives. He continued providing for her even after their divorce.

Rosemary was believed to protect people from evil spirits, lightning, and assault. It was also used as a love charm and to ensure success in any other endeavor. A tea made from rosemary leaves crushed in wine cured colds and improved the memory. Greek students would twine rosemary in their hair before examinations in the hope that it would help them remember what they had studied. Even today, rosemary wreaths are sometimes placed on the graves of soldiers to ensure that the living do not forget the sacrifice the soldiers have made.

If a rosemary plant unexpectedly appears in your garden, it is a sign that the woman of the house is strong, powerful, and intuitive. Her advice should always be taken seriously.

St. John's wort

St. John's wort was considered a magical plant everywhere it grew. It provided protection from ghosts, evil spirits, fire, and thunder and lightning. It was also used for love charms and to increase fertility.

St. John's wort is a yellow flower and its leaves contain red spots. These spots symbolize the blood of John the Baptist and were believed to appear each year on August 27th, as people believed he was beheaded on this day.

Young girls used to get up very early on St. John's Eve (June 23rd) to gather St. John's wort while the dew was still on the leaves. This ensured they would get married in the next twelve months. Unmarried women could induce a dream of their future husbands by sleeping with St. John's wort under their pillows. Barren women were advised to walk naked into their gardens on St. John's Eve to pick a flower of St. John's wort. This ensured they would have a baby within twelve months. Bonfires containing large amounts of St. John's wort were lit on St. John's Eve. Cattle were driven through the smoke to protect them from evil spirits. Charred branches of the shrub that had been smoked in the fire were kept and used as amulets to protect homes and other buildings.

Sunflower

The sunflower was brought to Europe from the Americas. The Spanish explorers called it *girasol*, which means "turn to the sun." Because the sunflower turns to face the sun, it became associated with devotion to God. The sunflower was sacred to the Incas who used it extensively in carvings and jewelry.

A Greek myth tells the story of a beautiful girl called Clytia who fell in love with Apollo, the sun god. Unfortunately, Apollo tired of the relationship and left her for another beautiful maiden called Leocothoe. Clytia told Leocothoe's father of the affair, which ensured she lost Apollo's love forever. Clytia, grief-stricken and in despair, pined away. The gods took pity on her and turned her into a sunflower. That meant she could continue to watch Apollo, the sun god, as he travels across the sky every day.

In China, the sunflower symbolized immortality, and people ate sunflower seeds in the hope of living long and happy lives.

Tulip

The ancient Persians considered the tulip a symbol of perfect love, and believed that it flowered in the gardens of paradise. Because the words for *tulip* and *Allah* were spelled with the same letters in Turkish, the flower became a symbol of divinity.

The tulip was introduced to Europe in the sixteenth century and became extremely popular in the Netherlands, where it symbolized beauty and wealth. Today the tulip is still used to symbolize the Netherlands.

Violet

An ancient myth tells of the death of Attis, who was killed while out hunting. Violets grew where his blood fell. The Greeks associated the violet with Io, who was one of many human women loved by Zeus. The ancient Romans wore violets, believing they prevented drunkenness. Gradually, thanks to Christian symbolism, the violet came to symbolize modesty and humility (which is where the term *shrinking violet* comes from).

Napoleon loved violets, and he used them to give hope to his followers. When he was exiled to Elba, he told his supporters that like the violets that return each spring, he too would return. His followers used the violet as their symbol, and Napoleon was affectionately known as "Caporal Violet." Napoleon gave a bunch of violets to Josephine on their wedding day. On their anniversary every year he gave her another bunch of violets. After she died he placed a violet from her grave into a locket, which he wore around his neck until his own death.

It is fortunate to dream of violets, as this is a sign that your circumstances are about to improve. A necklace made from violets prevents drunkenness and ensures you hear only the truth.

Yarrow

If a small posy of yarrow is offered to a newly married bride, the couple will enjoy conjugal happiness. As long as you carry a small sprig of yarrow, no one will be able to cast a spell on you.

four

Medicinal Plants

O, mickle is the powerful grace that lies
In plants, herbs, stones, and their true qualities;
For nought so vile that on earth doth live
But to the earth some special good doth give,
Within the infant rind of this weak flower
Poison hath residence and medicine power.

—Shakespeare, *Romeo and Juliet*, act 2, scene 3

*A*t one time virtually all medicines came from plants. Originally they were gathered in the wild, but it didn't take people long to discover the benefits of cultivating plants that could be used for medicinal purposes. All around the world, primitive people used plant medicines, and this knowledge was passed on through the generations in an oral tradition. Interestingly, animals also instinctively use plants as medicine. Dogs and cats, for instance, eat grass when they feel unwell.

The Papyrus Ebers can claim to be the world's oldest example of medical writing. This scroll is approximately 3,500 years old and was discovered in Luxor, Egypt in 1873 by Georg Ebers (1837–1898). The sixty-eight foot long scroll described the various illnesses and accidents suffered by people at that time. These included abscesses, burns, depression, problems in pregnancy, skin diseases, and skull fractures. There is even a cure for a crocodile bite. Some eight hundred remedies are included, many using plants such as caraway, cumin, fennel, licorice, and peppermint.

Licorice, incidentally, was also one of the oldest herbs used for medicinal purposes half a world away, in China. About 3000 BCE Emperor Shen Nung wrote the first Chinese book on medicine. In this book he mentioned licorice and thousands of other herbs, including ginseng, which he considered the most important. Ginseng is also mentioned in the *Atharva Veda*, the ancient book on Indian medicine. *The Shen Nung Herbal* (c. 200 BCE) was named after Emperor Shen Nung but was written approximately 2,800 years later. This work listed the medical applications of 365 plants, including the purgative *Ricinus communis* for asthma.[13]

The ancient Greeks and Romans made valuable contributions to medicine. In the first century CE, *De Materia Medica* by Dioscorides gave full details on planting, harvesting, and the medicinal uses of six hundred plants. This book became a standard textbook for hundreds of years. It was also translated into Arabic and Persian, where it inspired many later Islamic herbals. In the West, the herbals of John Gerard (1545–1612) and Nicholas Culpeper (1616–1654) owe a great deal to the pioneering work of Dioscorides.

During the Dark Ages in Europe, a number of herbals were produced. They were called "leechbooks" from the Anglo-Saxon *laece,* which means "to heal." These books contained numerous methods to ward off elves and other evil spirits. They also contained a great deal of herb and plant lore. The most famous of these books is the *Leechbook of Bald*, which dates from between 900 and 950 CE. Bald is believed to have been a friend of King Alfred the Great. According to his book, disease was caused by "elf-shot" or "flying venom." Because of this strong belief in evil forces, Bald's remedies were protective as well as restorative.

Monasteries became more powerful in medieval England after the invasion of William the Conqueror. Every monastery had an extensive herb garden, and the monks who looked after them were kept busy tending to sick people who needed their skill and expertise.

The *New Herball*, by William Turner, was published in parts between 1551 and 1562. It finally came out in book form in 1568, and was dedicated to Queen Elizabeth I. William Turner was a nonconformist and spent two years in prison for his views. He also had two lengthy periods of exile in Europe. This gave him time to research and work on his herbal. He continued with this project even after most early copies were destroyed during the reign of

---

13. John Mann, *Murder, Magic, and Medicine* (Oxford, UK: Oxford University Press, 1992), 111.

Queen Mary I. Fortunately, after her reign Turner was able to return to England and publish the remaining parts of his book during the more enlightened reign of Queen Elizabeth I. William Turner's book was extremely influential, and he is sometimes referred to as the "father of English botany."

Nicholas Culpeper's herbal, originally called *The English Physician Enlarged, with 369 Medicines Made of English Herbs*, was published in 1653, and revised versions of it can still be purchased today. Culpeper was a physician and astrologer, as well as a prolific author.

All around the world, people practiced herbal medicine. The early colonists of America brought their knowledge of medical remedies with them. The Native Americans gradually added to that knowledge by introducing a wide variety of new plants.

Many primitive cultures used hallucinogenic plants to gain access to the spirit world. Priests and shamans regularly used these plants, which they regarded as gifts from the gods, to gain insight into the future and to diagnose illnesses. These drugs were also sometimes used to stave off hunger pangs.

Today, herbal medicine is still widely practiced in Africa and much of Asia. Science is paying more attention to herbs and folk medicine than ever before. Drug companies, which stand to make millions of dollars from successful discoveries, are doing most of this research.

Arguably, the oldest medicine of all comes from the milky juice of the opium poppy (*Papaver somniferum*). Morphine and codeine, both of which diminish pain, are made from this juice.

Some plants could be used for most minor problems. Selfheal (*Prunella vulgaris*), as its name indicates, is a good example. Another commonly used plant was comfrey (*Symphytum officinale*), which grew wild beside roads and hedgerows. Every part of this plant was used for one purpose or another. It was used to treat wounds and broken bones, and to stop bleeding. It is also edible. However, comfrey can affect the liver, and I'd advise against taking it internally. Comfrey is still used as a medicinal plant today.

One explanation for the derivation of the name *foxglove* (*Digitalis purpurea*) is that people believed they would become as stealthy and cunning as a fox if they wore its flowers on their fingers. Another possibility is that *foxglove* is a contraction of "little folk's glove," since it is believed that you can contact nature spirits through this plant. The foxglove also warded off evil spirits, and was used to treat colds and fevers. During the eighteenth century, doctors discovered that foxglove stimulated the heart. Today, a drug called Digitalis, which is extracted from the purple foxglove, is used to treat a variety of heart conditions. The drugs Digitoxin and Digoxin are extracted from the white foxglove. Foxglove should be used with caution and should never be taken internally. It also causes dermatitis in some people, so it should not be worn in direct contact with the body.

Deadly nightshade (*Atropa belladonna*) was considered a magical plant. Although it was a well-known poison, it was also used as a medicine. Today the drug Atropine is made from it.

Mistletoe (*Viscum album*) has been considered magical since the days of the Druids, when mistletoe and vervain were the Druids' most important sacred plants. Mistletoe was used to attract good luck, and to protect homes and ward off evil spirits. It was commonly known as "all-heal," and was also used to increase fertility in both humans and animals.

Vervain (*Verbena officinalis*), the second most sacred plant to the Druids, was used to attract prosperity and to ward off evil. Vervain helped children learn more quickly. It was also extremely popular as an aphrodisiac.

The European mandrake (*Mandragora officinarum*) has been used for almost every possible magical purpose. This is because its roots resemble a human being, a fact that has both fascinated and terrified people. The plant could be harvested only at night, and three magic circles had to be created around it first to provide protection for the people extracting it. The European mandrake is highly poisonous and should be treated with great care. The American mandrake (*Podophyllum peltatum*) is less toxic, but it still needs to be treated with caution.

Quinine, at one time the only treatment for malaria, is an alkaloid that is found in the bark of the cinchona tree, which grows in the tropical forests of Bolivia and Peru. The Quechua Indians discovered it, and the Spanish conquistadors took it to Europe as a "miracle cure" in the sixteenth century.

Not very long ago, the cure for a headache was to chew on a piece of willow bark. Nowadays the aspirin you take for headaches is derived from salicylic acid—which, not surprisingly, comes from the bark of the white willow (*Salix alba*).

Cineol oil, which comes from the eucalyptus tree (*Eucalyptus globules*), is used to treat sore throats, bronchitis, and asthma.

Native Americans made a tea from the leaves of witch hazel (*Hamamelis virginiana*), which they used to wash infections and wounds. Today we know that witch hazel is a powerful antiseptic.

The maidenhair tree (*Ginkgo biloba*)—not the maidenhair fern—has been used by Chinese herbalists for thousands of years to treat a wide range of ailments. Today the leaves of the maidenhair tree are used to create medicines to improve blood circulation, especially to the brain.

Altogether, more than two thousand types of trees are used in the manufacture of medicines. Some are at the leading edge of research, such as the Australian Moreton Bay chestnut (*Castanospermum australe*), which produces an alkaloid that helps neutralize HIV.[14]

Few people gather wild flowers for medicinal purposes anymore. However, people are still making use of them as many pharmaceutical companies prepare medicines from flowers and sell them

---

14.   Tony Russell and Catherine Cutler, *The World Encyclopedia of Trees* (London: Lorenz Books, 2003), 42.

in prepackaged form. It has been estimated that between 30 and 40 percent of all prescription drugs are derived from plants.[15]

Homeopathy

Philippus Aureolus Theophrastus Bombastus von Hohenheim (1493–1541) achieved fame under the name of Paracelsus. He was a Swiss physician who was considered controversial in his day because he believed that a small amount of what makes people ill could also cure them.

Almost three hundred years later, Samuel Hahnemann (1755–1843), a German physician, found that a remedy for malaria, made from Peruvian cinchona tree bark, induced the symptoms of malaria in a healthy patient. Patients who took cinchona, the source of quinine, would sweat profusely, in exactly the same manner as patients suffering from malaria. Hahnemann then discovered that a minute amount of the same remedy would alleviate the symptoms. To his surprise, when he repeated the experiment both on himself and others, he found that the more diluted his doses became, the more effective the treatment. This marked the start of modern-day homeopathy, which is based on the ancient Greek idea that "like cures like." In other words, the symptoms of a disease could be considered the body's method of fighting the disease. Consequently, taking a minute amount of a remedy that creates the same symptoms of the disease will stimulate the person's defense mechanism to fight the disease.

Homeopaths create medicines from plants and dilute them many times until only the minutest trace of the original substance remains. This means that toxic plants such as deadly nightshade can be used for medicinal purposes. Because they are diluted so many times, homeopathic remedies work at an energetic level, helping the body to overcome stress and restore health.

---

15. Dr. Sarah Brewer, *Encyclopedia of Vitamins, Minerals and Herbal Supplements* (London: Constable and Robinson, 2002), xiv.

Bach Flower Remedies

One of the most interesting people in the history of the medicinal uses of flowers was an English physician named Edward Bach (1886–1936), who discovered the healing energies of selected plants and trees. In the 1930s, he pioneered the technique of creating healing tinctures by soaking a flower in water and exposing the preparation to heat or sunlight. This process imprints the essence of the flower into the water. The water is then strained and preserved in alcohol. The resulting essence has been demonstrated to restore people's mental and emotional equilibrium. This essence can be used on its own or with other healing systems.

Dr. Bach created thirty-eight different remedies that cover all of the emotions that we can experience. He is probably best known for his Rescue Remedy, which is found in home medicine cabinets around the world.

Flower essences treat the whole person rather than individual symptoms. They help people accept, acknowledge, forgive, and release long-held emotions, in order to enable healing to take place. They disempower and eliminate negative thought patterns and replace them with harmony and a more positive approach to life.

Dr. Bach wanted his essences to be as freely available as possible. At least forty companies around the world produce and market them, and many people gain pleasure, satisfaction, and benefit from making their own.

Edward Bach was born near Birmingham, in England. He was a humanitarian who had considered entering the church before deciding on medicine as a career. He soon noticed that although his patients' physical well-being was being attended to, nothing was being done to alleviate their stresses and anxieties. While studying bacteriology at University College Hospital, in London, he collapsed and after an operation was told he had three months to live. To everyone's surprise, he recovered and was soon back at work.

In 1919, while working at the London Homeopathic Hospital, Dr. Bach developed a range of vaccines for intestinal problems that are still being used today. These became known as the *seven Bach nosodes.* After observing the success of these, Dr. Bach noticed how similar types of people reacted in the same way to the different nosodes. This caused him to hypothesize that humanity was divided into a number of distinct personality types, which meant patients could be treated by observing their mental states as well as their physical problems.

In 1928, Dr. Bach started experimenting with three flowers: impatiens, clematis, and mimulus. The results were so promising that he gave up his medical practice to focus on discovering healing herbs that worked on different mental states.

In the eight years of life left to him, Dr. Bach completed his work on thirty-eight essences and set up the Bach Centre in Sotwell, Oxfordshire. His legacy was considerable. Dr. Bach's essences are used to provide emotional support for people, animals, and plants. They are often used on people with physical illnesses, but they work just on well with those suffering from emotional and mental stress.

The Bach Flower Remedies

Agrimony: This is for people who project an air of happiness while suffering inwardly. This remedy provides peace of mind.

Aspen: This is for people who fear something disastrous is about to happen. This remedy provides inner strength.

Beech: This is for people who are intolerant and critical of others. This remedy makes them more tolerant.

Centaury: This is for people who find it hard to say no, and who are easily pushed around by others. This remedy helps them stand up for themselves.

Cerato: This is for people who doubt their own judgment and rely on the advice of others. This remedy helps them trust their own inner wisdom.

Cherry plum: This is for people who find it hard to control their thoughts. This remedy provides hope.

Chestnut bud: This is for people who find it hard to learn from experience, and who constantly make the same mistakes. This remedy helps relieve repetitive thoughts.

Chicory: This is for people who are overly possessive and dominating. This remedy helps them look inside themselves for what they are searching for.

Clematis: This is for people who are dreamy, inattentive, absent-minded, and indifferent. This remedy helps them to be more attentive and better organized.

Crabapple: This is for people who feel unclean and hate themselves. This remedy helps them see life as it really is.

Elm: This is for people who feel overwhelmed, inadequate, and unable to cope. This remedy helps them gain strength and confidence in their abilities and worth.

Gentian: This is for people who are easily discouraged. This remedy helps them see life from a different perspective.

Gorse: This is for people who are in a state of despair and despondency. This remedy provides feelings of hope and optimism.

Heather: This is for people who are totally consumed by their own problems. This remedy enables them to feel more positive and outgoing.

Holly: This is for people who suffer from negativity, jealousy, envy, and hatred. This remedy provides love and harmony.

Honeysuckle: This is for people who suffer from nostalgia and who dwell in the past. This remedy enables them to live in the present and look forward to the future.

Hornbeam: This is for people who procrastinate and find it hard to start anything. This remedy clears the mind and instills motivation.

Impatiens: This is for people who are irritable and impatient. This remedy provides patience and understanding.

Larch: This is for people who lack confidence, feel inferior, and expect to fail. This remedy helps them gain confidence and self-esteem.

Mimulus: This is for people who suffer from shyness and timidity. This remedy provides courage and inner strength.

Mustard: This is for people who suffer from melancholy, gloominess, and depression. This remedy encourages feelings of happiness and joy.

Oak: This is for people who constantly struggle and persevere, despite constant setbacks. This remedy provides them with the necessary strength to do what they have to do.

Olive: This is for people who are lacking in energy and feel constantly tired. This remedy helps them gain strength and energy.

Pine: This is for people who feel unworthy and suffer constant guilt. This remedy eliminates unhealthy patterns of thought.

Red chestnut: This is for people who are overly concerned about others, especially loved ones. This remedy helps them overcome negative thoughts and feelings.

Rockrose: This is for people who feel scared and fearful. This remedy helps them feel calm, positive, and in control of their lives.

Rock water: This is for people who are overly rigid and deny themselves pleasure. Rock water is not a flower essence, but it is water taken from a natural spring. This remedy helps people go with the flow of life.

Scleranthus: This is for people who suffer from uncertainty and indecision. This remedy helps them regain control of their thoughts.

Star of Bethlehem: This is for people who are suffering from fright or sudden stress. This remedy helps rebalance the nervous system.

Sweet chestnut: This is for people who feel totally dejected. This remedy provides comfort and support.

Vervain: This is for people who are highly-strung and attempt too much. This remedy helps them regain a sense of proportion.

Vine: This is for people who are domineering, inflexible, and overly ambitious. This remedy helps them gain understanding of the needs of others.

Walnut: This is for people who are experiencing major changes or adjustments in their lives. This remedy provides protection from any negative forces.

Water violet: This is for people who are reliable, reserved, and cautious but find it hard to express their emotions. This remedy helps them become more involved in their lives.

White chestnut: This is for people who are preoccupied with unwanted concerns, worries, and thoughts. This remedy helps eliminate worry.

Wild oat: This is for people who are trying to find their correct path in life. This remedy helps them discover their true path.

Wild rose: This is for people who are apathetic, resigned, and lacking in ambition. This remedy helps them regain lost enthusiasm and energy.

Willow: This is for people who are full of resentment, bitterness, and self-pity. This remedy helps them forgive and look at life with new optimism.

Rescue Remedy is sometimes considered the thirty-ninth remedy. A mixture of cherry plum, clematis, impatiens, rockrose, and star of Bethlehem, it is an all-purpose remedy for anyone suffering from shock, fear, panic, emotional upset, stage fright, or facing a stressful situation such as an examination or a dentist appointment.

Aromatherapy

Aromatherapy is the art and science of using natural aromatic oils to facilitate healing. Essential oils are complex substances obtained from the fruits, flowers, bark, roots, or resins of aromatic plants and trees. A good example of an essential oil is the tangy, citrus scent released from an orange when you peel it. Another example is the relaxing smell of a freshly mown lawn.

You are practicing aromatherapy in its simplest form when you take an ill friend a bouquet of pleasant-smelling flowers. Roses are a good example. The delicate perfume provides feelings of happiness and well-being that lifts the spirits of the patient.

The ancient Egyptians practiced a form of aromatherapy. While excavating long forgotten tombs, archaeologists discovered numerous urns that had contained essential oils. The Egyptians used essential oils for religious purposes, for embalming dead bodies, for beautifying themselves, and for medicinal purposes.

At the start of the twentieth century, Dr. R. M. Gattefossé (1881–1950), a French chemist, coined the word *aromatherapy* and wrote several books on essential oils and how they should be used. His interest in the subject began when he accidentally burned his hand in his laboratory and plunged it into the nearest container of liquid, which happened to be oil of lavender. He was amazed at how quickly the pain disappeared and his hand healed. He used his knowledge and skill to help injured soldiers in World War I.

Although people continued experimenting with aromatherapy in the 1930s and 1940s, modern day aromatherapy really began in the 1950s when Marguerite Maury (1895–1968), an Austrian-born French biochemist, started blending oils specifically for the needs of individuals. Almost single-handedly, she reestablished aromatherapy as a subject worthy of study.

Aromatherapy is a holistic treatment that works on the entire body rather than a specific ailment. The oil is either inhaled through the nose or absorbed through the skin, usually in a bath or in the course of a massage.

More than one hundred essential oils are used in aromatherapy, but less than half of them are used for most purposes. Here are some of the most useful essential oils:

(Pregnant women should not use basil, bay, comfrey, cypress, fennel, geranium, hyssop, juniper, marjoram, myrrh, rosemary, sage, or thyme.)

Basil

There are more than one hundred varieties of basil. It originated in India and reached Europe in the sixteenth century. The Romans prized basil, which they considered an aphrodisiac.

Basil relieves bronchitis, colds, and indigestion. It helps eliminate fatigue, anxieties, worries, depression, and insomnia.

Basil also stimulates sexual activity. Dried basil under a bed can reawaken the passion in a relationship.

Bay

Bay is a popular culinary herb that aids digestion and acts as a tonic for the system. It relieves bronchitis, colds, and influenza. It is also used as a remedy for baldness.

The ancient Greeks crowned their winners with bay, making it a symbol of success.

Benzoin

Benzoin relieves urinary infections, skin problems such as eczema and psoriasis, and respiratory problems such as coughs and colds. Benzoin is also useful for relieving bedsores, skin ulcers, and even frostbite.

Bergamot

Bergamot is an effective antiseptic that aids sore throats and skin infections. It is also used as a cure for indigestion. Bergamot is used extensively in the cosmetic industry, and many soaps and perfumes are made with it.

Cedarwood

Cedarwood is effective in treating many skin problems such as acne, alopecia, psoriasis, dandruff, eczema, and rashes. It is also used as a diuretic. Cedarwood also works on the mind, relieving long-term anxieties and worries.

Chamomile

Chamomile is an excellent antiseptic and was used for this purpose until the late 1940s. Today it is used for many purposes including allergies, dermatitis, diarrhea, fever, gout, hay fever, headaches, indigestion, insomnia, neuralgia, rheumatism, and toothaches. Chamomile tea calms the nerves and reduces tension. It also raises the spirits and creates feelings of well-being.

Cinnamon

Cinnamon is an effective remedy for over-tiredness and depression. It is also a tonic that aids coughs, colds, influenza, and stomachaches. It stimulates the digestive system. Cinnamon is used as an aphrodisiac, and some people claim it can cure impotence.

Clary sage

Clary sage is particularly useful for stress-related problems. It raises people's spirits and enables them to think in a more positive manner. It is also used to help people with menstrual problems, abdominal cramps, and sore throats.

Clove

Clove is a stimulant that aids digestion and restores the appetite. It is useful for mouth infections and it soothes toothache. It is good for the immune system, and helps alleviate physical and mental strain. In both China and Japan, clove symbolizes sweetness and good health. In Japanese art, clove is frequently depicted with the Seven Deities of Good Fortune.

Comfrey

Comfrey is particularly useful as a treatment for wounds and skin problems, including athlete's foot, eczema, and psoriasis. It is also used for stretch marks and menstrual problems.

Cypress

Cypress is used for treating coughs, colds, hemorrhoids, menstrual problems, and varicose veins. It is also used to soothe stress and nervous tension. It can help relieve menopausal symptoms, too.

Eucalyptus

Eucalyptus is an antiseptic, and is widely used as a cure for coughs, colds, influenza, rheumatism, muscular aches, and viral infections. It is used to help treat asthma, bronchitis, and skin infections.

Fennel

Fennel is a diuretic that can help relieve colic, constipation, digestive problems, and nausea. It can provide additional energy for people engaged in physical activities and provide strength for those convalescing after an illness. It is also used to alleviate conjunctivitis and puffiness around the eyes.

Frankincense

Frankincense aids in concentration and raises the spirits. It is also used as an expectorant to help relieve bronchitis, coughs, and laryngitis. Frankincense also aids meditation.

Garlic

Garlic has been used as a medicine since Egyptian times. They included it in the diet to ensure strength and good health. It was also used to treat headaches, insomnia, and infections. Athletes in Greece and Rome chewed garlic to increase their chances of success. In European folklore, garlic also provides supernatural protection and at one time was used to ward off werewolves and vampires.

Geranium

Geranium is one of the most useful of all aromatherapy oils. It helps people overcome fatigue and speeds up recovery from lengthy illnesses. It is useful for nervous disorders and depression. It is also used for skin problems such as athlete's foot, fungal infections, and sores. It also can be used as a highly effective insect repellent.

Hyssop

Hyssop helps regulate blood pressure. It is also used to help cure bronchial problems and skin conditions. A poultice of hyssop relieves bruises, cuts, and wounds.

Jasmine

Jasmine creates feelings of well-being and eliminates anxiety. It is used as an aphrodisiac and is reputed to be a cure for both impotence and frigidity. It is also used to alleviate infections in the eyes. Jasmine tea, which is a mixture of Chinese green tea and dried jasmine leaves, works as a stimulant, making people feel more positive about their lives.

Juniper

Juniper works as a diuretic and antiseptic. It helps treat acne, coughs, cystitis, flatulence, joint problems, and rheumatism. Juniper is also used to flavor gin.

Lavender

Lavender balances the emotional and nervous systems, and is extremely versatile. It is a remedy for headaches and migraines. It is an antiseptic that aids skin problems and has proven especially useful for burn victims. It is also used for acne, bruises, dermatitis, and oily skin.

Lemon

Lemon works well on skin problems, as it is both an antiseptic and an astringent. It is a popular cure for bronchitis, colds, coughs, and sore throats. It also lowers blood pressure, and helps treat fevers and digestive problems. It can also help people suffering from insomnia.

Lemongrass

Lemongrass is used to treat athlete's foot, colitis, flatulence, headaches, respiratory problems, and skin disorders. It also aids digestion.

Marjoram

Marjoram is used to treat a variety of problems, including anxiety, arthritis, asthma, constipation, insomnia, menstrual problems, migraines, and rheumatism. It also relieves nervous tension.

Myrrh

Myrrh was highly prized by the ancient Greeks and Egyptians. It is used to heal skin problems such as acne and dermatitis. It is also useful for skin ulcers and infections. In addition, myrrh can be used to treat bronchitis, coughs, colds, and influenza.

Neroli

Neroli is distilled from the flowers of the Seville orange and is named after an Italian princess who loved the perfume. Neroli works as an antidepressant and is used to treat anxiety, shock, and stress. It is also a sedative that is used to cure insomnia.

Orange

Orange can lift feelings of anxiety, hopelessness, and depression. It stimulates the appetite and cures constipation. Its antiseptic qualities make it an effective treatment for mouth ulcers. It also rejuvenates the skin and helps it regain its youthful vitality.

Parsley

Parsley is a good diuretic, and is used for kidney and urinary problems. It also relieves tired or sore eyes and helps with menstrual problems. It is also an excellent aid for digestion.

Patchouli

Patchouli is used to treat skin conditions such as abscesses, acne, cracked skin, dandruff, dermatitis, eczema, and scars on the skin. It creates feelings of happiness and well-being. Consequently, it is sometimes used to treat anxiety and depression.

Peppermint

Peppermint is highly versatile and is used to aid the digestion and treat skin problems. It is also used for colds, flatulence, headaches, indigestion, nausea, and sunburn.

Pine

Pine is a good antiseptic. It is used to treat respiratory problems, such as bronchitis, colds, influenza, and sinusitis. It is also used to relieve rheumatism and muscular pains.

Rose

Rose is uplifting and positive. It makes an effective aphrodisiac, and is also used to treat constipation, headaches, menstrual and menopausal problems, and circulation problems.

Rosemary

Rosemary is used to treat a variety of ailments including alopecia, asthma, colds, dandruff, diarrhea, headaches, obesity, and rheumatism. Rosemary makes a highly effective hair tonic. Students in ancient Greece wore rosemary to improve their concentration and memory. They also associated it with love and long-lasting relationships.

Sage

Sage is a natural deodorant. It calms the mind, enabling clear thought and planning. Sage is used to treat bronchitis, bacterial infections, colds, headaches, rheumatism, and water retention. The ancient Greeks associated sage with wisdom and immortality. Sage derives its name from *salvus*, a Latin word meaning "to be in good health." European herbalists considered sage a cure for almost everything.

Sandalwood

Sandalwood is considered an aphrodisiac; it also raises the spirits and alleviates depression. It is also used to treat bronchitis and skin conditions.

Tea tree

Tea tree is an excellent disinfectant and germicide. It is used to treat skin conditions such as acne, athlete's foot, burns, cold sores, verrucas, and warts. It is one of the very few essential oils that can be used undiluted as an antiseptic on broken skin. It is also useful for gynecological problems and infections of the ears, nose, and mouth.

Thyme

Thyme is an excellent antiseptic that is used for coughs, colds, and respiratory infections. It can also relieve the pain of backaches, rheumatism, and sciatica. Thyme is a stimulant and can raise the spirits of people suffering from anxiety or depression.

Ylang-ylang

Ylang-ylang is soothing and relaxing. It is used to treat anxiety, depression, frigidity, and insomnia. It can help nervous people gain more confidence in themselves.

Aromatherapy in the Bath

Essential oils can be used in a number of ways. Six to eight drops of oil added to a bath create a wonderful, relaxing, tension-releasing bath. You can use one, two, or three essential oils in your bath to create the right combination. Stir the bathwater after adding the oils to disperse the molecules throughout the bath. If you wish, you can add to the mood by lighting candles and playing relaxing music. Stay as long as you wish in the bath, enjoying the perfume and warm water. After the bath, pat your skin dry—as doing so leaves a small amount of essential oil on your skin where it can be absorbed.

My favorite combination of oils for a relaxing bath is two drops of orange, two drops of sandalwood, and four drops of patchouli.

Enjoying a fragrant bath with a friend is one of the best ways I've found to relax after a stressful day.

Vaporizer

Ceramic vaporizers can be found at most New Age stores and gift shops. They usually consist of a candle holder beneath a shallow dish. Water and a few drops of oil are placed in the dish, and the candle is lit. As the oil evaporates the scent is absorbed and almost instantly affects the person's mind and spirit. Depending on the oils you choose, you can create almost any mood or feeling you desire. Four drops of myrrh, three drops of frankincense, and two drops of pine oil create a tranquil, spiritual atmosphere that is perfect for quiet meditation or contemplation. Conversely, a cheerful, social atmosphere can be created with three drops each of orange, peppermint, and clary sage.

Massage

Essential oils are too concentrated to be used directly on the skin. Consequently, they must be added to a massage base oil to create a wonderfully healing and beneficial oil for a massage. Massage base oils are made from vegetables, nuts, or seeds, which can be beneficial on their own but gain added potency when mixed with essential oils. I like wheat germ, avocado, and olive oils. My wife likes jojoba oil as it is a highly effective skin moisturizer. Prepare the massage oil by pouring half an ounce of base oil into a small container and adding seven or eight drops in total of your selected essential oils. You may need an ounce of base oil if massaging a large person.

It can be a wonderfully relaxing experience for two people to take turns massaging each other. You can also nurture yourself with a self-massage. One of the joys of aromatherapy is the opportunity it provides for experimentation. You can create a different blend every day if you wish.

Inhalation

When I was a child my mother prepared an aromatherapy mixture whenever we had a sore throat. Her mixture contained eucalyptus and peppermint oils. I recall she also used cedarwood with eucalyptus to relieve congested lungs.

Half fill a stainless steel bowl with almost boiling water. Add a few drops of your chosen oil or oils, stirring them into the water. Place a towel over your head, close your eyes, and breathe deeply over the bowl for several minutes.

This method can also be used to eliminate stress, fear, and worry. Add three drops each of frankincense and myrrh into the hot water, stir, place a towel over your head, and breathe deeply for several minutes.

Foot Bath

You can create a relaxing foot bath by adding five or six drops of essential oil to a bowl of warm to hot water. Mix the oil into the water and then soak your feet in the bath for fifteen to twenty minutes.

Perfume

Add a few drops of essential oil or oils to a handkerchief or cotton pad and place it in a pocket. You will find the delicate fragrance will affect your mind, body, and spirit. If you wish, you can also inhale the fragrance directly from the handkerchief.

• • •

Bach flowers and aromatherapy also play a role in astrology. We will look at this, and more, in the next chapter.

five

Plants and Astrology

*P*lants have always been associated with different months and seasons.

People believed they would receive good luck if they wore the blossom associated with their birth month. Unfortunately, various flowers have been suggested at different times; it is impossible to list a single flower for each month. Here are the most popular choices:

January: snowdrop (purity) or carnation (protection and courage)
February: violet (gentleness and spirituality)
March: daffodil (sincerity)
April: primrose (rebirth and love) or sweet pea (versatility)
May: white lily (fortitude) or lily of the valley (optimism)
June: wild rose (love and healing)
July: carnation (protection) or delphinium (health and happiness)
August: white heather (good fortune) or poppy (renewal)
September: Michaelmas daisy (happiness) or aster (elegance)
October: rosemary (benevolence) or marigold (happiness)
November: chrysanthemum (insights)
December: ivy (faithfulness) or holly (strength, resilience, and renewal)

From this, it was only a short step to relating various flowers to the different signs of the zodiac. In the seventeenth century, Nicholas Culpeper combined astrology, diseases, and plants in his book *The English Physician, or Herball.* This book became extremely popular because people found it easy to decide which medicinal plants to use.

The Bach flowers listed for each sign will enhance the good qualities of the sign, while alleviating some of the negative qualities.

The suggested aromatherapy oils can be used as a perfume to help attract the right person to you. You can use either the oil that relates to your sign or the oil that relates to the sign of the person you are hoping to attract.

You may find you have an association with the plants that relate to your horoscope sign. Many people plant flowers and trees relating to their sun sign, which they believe they will protect their home.

Aries

Birth flower: honeysuckle and sweet pea
Other flowers: gorse, nasturtium, peppermint, and thistle
Trees: chestnut, holly, and thorn
Bach flower: impatiens
Aromatherapy oils: cinnamon and rosemary
Ruler: Mars
Lucky day: Tuesday
Element: fire

Aries are impulsive, enthusiastic, mentally alert, and full of new ideas. They make natural leaders. They can be quick-tempered at times, but are unable to hold grudges for long.

Arians working on the negative side of their potential are impatient, egocentric, and inconsiderate. Plants that can help them overcome these traits include blackberry, heather, impatiens, and sunflower.

Plants and flowers you should consider sending to an Arian include amaryllis, daisies, prickly pear, red peppers, poppies, red roses, tiger lilies, and tulips. Arians like large bouquets with large, preferably red flowers.

Taurus

Birth flower: foxglove, poppy, and rose
Other flowers: columbine, daisy, primula, and violet
Trees: almond, apple, ash, cherry, fig, pear, and walnut
Bach flower: gentian
Aromatherapy oil: rose
Ruler: Venus
Lucky day: Friday
Element: earth

Taureans are reliable, stable, persistent, and stubborn. They are patient, careful, and appreciate all the good things of life. They enjoy money, quality, comfort, and security.

Taureans working on the negative side of their potential are apathetic and demonstrate a fixed approach to life. Plants that can help them overcome these traits include gentian, iris, and wild rose.

Plants and flowers you should consider sending to a Taurean include aster, lavender, lilac, lilies (especially lilies of the valley and stargazer lilies), and sweet William. Taureans appreciate all flowers as long as they are given with love.

Gemini

Birth flower: lavender and lily of the valley
Other flowers: iris, myrtle, and snapdragon
Trees: chestnut, elder, and hazel
Bach flower: cerato
Aromatherapy oil: cedarwood
Ruler: Mercury
Lucky day: Wednesday
Element: air

Geminis are affectionate, sympathetic, charming, and easy to get along with. They possess quick, restless minds, which they enjoy exercising in conversation. They enjoy being busy, and frequently do more than one thing at a time.

Geminis working on the negative side of their potential are overly anxious worriers with endless inner chatter going on in their minds. Plants that can help them overcome these traits include white chestnut, morning glory, and lavender.

Plants and flowers you should consider sending to a Gemini include acacia, cactus, chrysanthemum, daffodil, maidenhair fern, narcissus, ranunculus, and red roses. Geminis like flowers and will be thrilled with whatever you give them.

Cancer

> **Birth flower:** white rose and larkspur
> **Other flowers:** convolvulus, geranium, lily, and water lily
> **Trees:** maple, sycamore, and willow
> **Bach flower:** clematis
> **Aromatherapy oil:** gardenia
> **Ruler:** Moon
> **Lucky day:** Monday
> **Element:** water

Cancerians are quiet, sensitive, and emotional. They are versatile and possess good imaginations. They have a strong love for home and family, and enjoy being surrounded by loved ones.

Cancerians working on the negative side of their potential are emotionally needy and overly protective and anxious about loved ones. Plants that can help them overcome these traits include chamomile, chicory, clematis, and honeysuckle.

Plants and flowers you should consider sending to a Cancerian include cornflower, delphinium, ferns, hydrangea, iris, lily, passionflower, and white roses. Cancerians love receiving flowers and will remember the gift—and the individual flowers you chose—for years.

Leo

> **Birth flower:** marigold and sunflower
> **Other flowers:** cowslip, forsythia, heliotrope, passionflower, and peony
> **Trees:** bay, citrus trees, laurel, oak, olive, and pine
> **Bach flower:** vervain
> **Aromatherapy oils:** neroli, patchouli, and sandalwood
> **Ruler:** Sun
> **Lucky day:** Sunday
> **Element:** fire

Leos are generous, optimistic, independent, and outgoing. They are friendly and enjoy receiving gratitude and appreciation from others. Leos are easy to get along with when everything is going their way. They are quick to anger but just as quick to let it go.

Leos working on the negative side of their potential are inflexible, intolerant, egocentric, and overdemanding. Plants that can help them overcome these traits include borage, dandelion, iris, and vervain.

Plants and flowers you should consider giving a Leo include croton, dahlia, gerbera, gladioli, Joseph's coat, and safflower. Leos enjoy receiving large bouquets containing large and preferably exotic flowers.

Virgo

Birth flower: buttercup and pansy
Other flowers: cornflower, Madonna lily, and rosemary
Trees: elder, hazel, and all nut-bearing trees
Bach flower: centaury
Aromatherapy oils: orange and rose
Ruler: Mercury
Lucky day: Wednesday
Element: earth

Virgos are modest, thoughtful, serious, and orderly. They are inclined to be perfectionists. They are idealistic but keep their feet on the ground. They enjoy learning and seek to improve their minds.

Virgos working on the negative side of their potential are overly critical and judgmental. Plants that can help them overcome these traits include beech, dill, jasmine, self-heal, and zinnia.

Plants and flowers you should consider sending to a Virgo include aster, chrysanthemum, daisies, eucalyptus, blue hydrangea, ivy, hypericum (St. John's wort), and violet. As Virgo is a highly practical sign, a gift of a carefully chosen potted plant will be greatly appreciated.

Libra

Birth flower: bluebell and rose
Other flowers: apple blossom, hydrangea, and love-in-a-mist
Trees: almond, apple, ash, myrtle, plum, poplar, and walnut
Bach flower: scleranthus
Aromatherapy oil: jasmine
Ruler: Venus
Lucky day: Friday
Element: air

Libras are affectionate, agreeable, sympathetic people. They make natural peacemakers, as they enjoy harmony and can see both sides of a situation. The symbol for Libra is the scales, and it is an appropriate one since Libras always seek balance.

Libras working on the negative side of their potential are indecisive and overly emotional. Plants that can help them overcome these traits include clover, eucalyptus, holly, and sweet pea.

Plants and flowers you should consider sending to a Libra include bonsai plants, cymbidium orchids, freesia, gardenia, gladioli, miniature roses, and tulips. Libras like to receive bouquets containing many pink and white flowers. It is important that the bouquet is tasteful and beautifully presented.

Scorpio

Birth flower: geranium and chrysanthemum
Other flowers: basil, purple heather, and rhododendron
Trees: blackthorn and holly
Bach flower: chicory
Aromatherapy oils: cumin and ylang-ylang
Ruler: Mars
Lucky day: Tuesday
Element: water

Scorpios are shrewd, intense, secretive, and determined. They possess a great deal of drive and determination. They can be critical and skeptical, and they express their views in a direct manner.

Scorpios working on the negative side of their potential are suspicious, resentful, and unforgiving. Plants that can help them overcome these traits include basil, fuchsia, gorse, holly, and honeysuckle.

Plants and flowers you should consider sending to a Scorpio include amaranthus, cactus, carnations, chrysanthemum, hibiscus, lily, peony, red-hot poker, and Venus flytrap. Scorpios like receiving bouquets of red flowers such as carnations, chrysanthemums, and roses.

Sagittarius

Birth flower: carnation and narcissus
Other flowers: dandelion, sage, thistle, and wallflower
Trees: ash, birch, chestnut, mulberry, oak, and vine
Bach flower: agrimony
Aromatherapy oil: gardenia
Ruler: Jupiter
Lucky day: Thursday
Element: fire

Sagittarians are positive, enthusiastic, and ambitious. They are sincere and honorable but frequently express themselves without thinking of the consequences.

Sagittarians working on the negative side of their potential are overly expansive and unrealistically optimistic. Flowers to help them overcome these traits include agrimony, borage, sage, and zinnia.

Plants and flowers you should consider sending to a Sagittarius include allium, blazing star, carnation, chrysanthemum, crocus, purple gladioli, foxtail lily, lavender roses, and tulips. Sagittarians like receiving bouquets of red and white flowers.

Capricorn

Birth flower: carnation, ivy, and pansy
Other flowers: amaranthus, nightshade, rue, and snowdrop
Trees: cypress, elm, holly, pine, poplar, spruce, willow, and yew
Bach flower: mimulus
Aromatherapy oil: jasmine
Ruler: Saturn
Lucky day: Saturday
Element: earth

Capricorns are practical, thoughtful, persistent, and patient. They invariably reach their goals because they hang on indomitably until their goals are realized.

Capricorns working on the negative side of their potential are despondent, pessimistic, and stubborn. Plants that can help them overcome these traits include aspen, blackberry, borage, elm, and oak.

Plants and flowers you should consider sending to a Capricorn include African violet, bluebell, carnation, holly, ivy, jasmine, philodendron, poinsettia, and snowdrop. Capricorns enjoy receiving simple bouquets containing bluebells, carnations, chrysanthemums, and tulips.

Aquarius

Birth flower: orchid
Other flowers: foxglove, gentian violet, and snowdrop
Trees: all fruit trees and pine
Bach flower: water violet
Aromatherapy oils: coriander and nutmeg
Ruler: Uranus
Lucky day: Saturday
Element: air

Aquarians are tolerant, sympathetic, and understanding people who make natural humanitarians. They are usually more concerned with humanity as a whole rather than individuals. Aquarians often have an interest in offbeat or unusual subjects.

Aquarians working on the negative side of their potential are aloof, superior, and supercilious. Plants that can help them overcome these traits include chamomile, dandelion, dill, vervain, and violet.

Plants and flowers you should consider sending to an Aquarian include arum lily, banksias, bird of paradise, gladioli, iris, orchids, protea, and yucca. Aquarians love anything fresh, different, or exotic. Send them a bouquet of unusual flowers.

Pisces

Birth flower: water lily and jonquil
Other flowers: carnation, heliotrope, poppy, and violet
Trees: fig and willow, plus all trees growing close to water
Bach flower: rockrose
Aromatherapy oils: narcissus and sage
Ruler: Neptune
Lucky day: Thursday
Element: water

Pisceans are kind, loving, and trusting. They are idealistic, imaginative, and emotional people who find it hard to make decisions. They are generally neat and tidy.

Pisceans working on the negative side of their potential are overly sensitive, dreamy, and unworldly. Plants that can help them overcome these traits include angelica, clematis, forget-me-not, lotus, and morning glory.

Plants and flowers you should consider sending to a Piscean include daffodils, forget-me-nots, gypsophila, jasmine, lilac, Madonna lily, narcissus, and roses. Pisceans are sensitive and romantic. Bouquets can be of any size as long as they are given with love. Blue and violet flowers are especially appreciated.

The Planets

The positions of the planets at the time of birth are one of the most important factors in astrology. The planets are placed in houses and signs, which an astrologer can interpret to determine the character and potential of the individual. The movements of the planets through the signs and houses, and the different relationships this creates, can also be interpreted to predict future trends in the person's life.

Traditionally, there were seven planets: Sun, Moon, Mercury, Venus, Mars, Jupiter, and Saturn. Astrologers today also include Uranus, Neptune and Pluto, but these planets were not known to astrologers of the past.

Sun

Zodiac sign: Leo
Colors: yellow, orange, and gold
Tree: oak
The sun takes a year to pass through all twelve signs of the zodiac. Consequently, the plants associated with it are usually annuals, such as calendula, cinnamon, sassafras, and sunflower.

Moon

Zodiac sign: Cancer
Colors: white, cream, and silver
Tree: walnut
Plants associated with the moon usually resemble it in some way. Pumpkins and melons are good examples.

Mercury

Zodiac signs: Gemini and Virgo

Colors: yellow, orange, and purple

Tree: olive

As Mercury relates to the element of air, the plants associated with it often contain divided leaves or stalks. Anise seeds, coriander, fenugreek seeds, licorice roots, and sweet marjoram are all related to Mercury.

Venus

Zodiac signs: Taurus and Libra

Colors: green and pink

Tree: myrtle

Venus is the planet of beauty, and the plants related to it contain fruits and a pleasing fragrance. Examples include blackberry, wild cherry, motherwort, and raspberry.

Mars

Zodiac signs: Aries and Scorpio

Colors: strong, vibrant reds

Tree: holly

Mars is the planet of aggression, and plants associated with it are red in color and possess thorns. Examples include barberry berries, hawthorn, and sarsaparilla.

Jupiter

Zodiac signs: Sagittarius and Pisces

Colors: blue and purple

Tree: birch

The plants associated with Jupiter are large and frequently contain an aspect that reminds people of the cross of Jesus. Examples include clove, fig, myrrh, nutmeg, and sage.

Saturn

Zodiac signs: Capricorn and Aquarius

Colors: black, gray, dark brown

Tree: yew

Woody perennials relate to Saturn. These include chamomile, linden flowers, black poppy seeds, and thistle.

• • •

In the next chapter we'll look at shamanism, one of the oldest spiritual practices in the world.

six

Shamanism

*S*hamanism has been practiced almost everywhere from Australia to Siberia, from Japan to Africa. Shamans are the healers, priests, rainmakers, and magicians who tend the sick, conduct rituals, and attend to the spiritual well-being of the community. The word *shaman* comes from the Tungus language of Siberia and means "he who knows."

At the heart of shamanism is the belief that everything, inanimate or living, possesses a spirit. Consequently, when a hunter kills a lion, for instance, he must also somehow appease the spirit of the animal. Likewise, the spirit of a tree has to be appeased before the tree is chopped down.

Most shamanic societies have a concept of three worlds, which are connected by a giant tree. The three worlds are the Underworld, the everyday world we live in, and the sky world, or heaven. Spirits inhabit all three worlds. Shamans are able to travel from one world to another by visualizing the connecting tree and allowing their soul to travel along it. This is called *soul flight*.

Shamans have the ability to send their souls on spiritual journeys to communicate with other spirits and to communicate with the gods. Sometimes these journeys occur spontaneously, while at other times an altered state of consciousness is necessary. Drumming, chanting, and dancing are all effective ways to enter the required trance state. Sacred plants are also frequently used. Shamans in Europe might use psilocybe mushrooms or fly agaric, while peyote is the drug of choice in Central America. In the Amazon, ayahuasca is used. Shamans in Bolivia and Peru use a drink made from the sap of the San Pedro cactus. Datura is used in Hawaii and Mexico. An alcoholic drink made from maguey cactus is also used in Mexico. Every part of the world has its own consciousness-altering plants.

Reindeers in Lapland are the only animals that deliberately intoxicate themselves with the fly-agaric mushroom. This makes them easy to handle and enables the Laplanders to work with them. The popular story of Santa Claus and his reindeer may well be a recounting of the shamanic journey, especially since Santa's costume has the same colors—red and white—as the magic mushroom.

These hallucinogenic plants enable the shaman to travel to other worlds and to communicate telepathically with spirits and gods. Naturally, in the shamanic worldview every aspect of nature contains spirits that can be communicated with in order to gain insight, understanding, and help. Consequently, shamans regularly communicate with plant spirits, especially for healing purposes.

Shamanism is still practiced in many parts of the world. Although there may seem little place for shamanism in the Western world, aspects of it, such as intimacy with nature, still play a vital role in helping people achieve peace of mind and spiritual growth, no matter where they happen to live.

Plant Spirits

The Mestizo people of Peru believe that every species of plant has a unique song. If you become especially close to a plant and listen carefully, you may hear the song while in a dream or daydream. Each song contains the healing energy of the plant it came from. Singing the song allows the healing energy of the plant to help others.

Ten thousand years before Dr. Edward Bach discovered his flower essences, the Aboriginal people of Australia were using flower essences. They believed that dewdrops found on the petals of flowers in the morning were magically filled with the flower's healing spirit, and could be used for medicinal purposes.[16]

Sacred Space

I've been fortunate enough to visit many sacred and spiritual sites around the world. The spirituality and energy created by some of these sites over hundreds, and sometimes thousands, of years is

---

16. Clare G. Harvey and Amanda Cochrane, *The Healing Spirit of Plants* (New York: Sterling, 1999), 24–25.

remarkable. However, the most sacred site I'm aware of is in a nature reserve, about a ten-minute walk away from my home. It's my own sacred space where I go to meditate, conduct rituals, relax, and recharge my spiritual energies (see chapter 13). I always return home restored in mind, body, and soul.

I've always enjoyed walking, and I especially enjoy exploring wild and remote places where I can pause and admire a tree, a flower, or even a leaf. I also find it highly restorative to watch cloud formations, flights of birds, and the busyness of insects. As a modern-day shaman, it is important to take time to relate to the natural world.

There are also other benefits from communing with nature. Mind, a British mental-health organization, considers ecotherapy—restoring health by spending time with nature—an effective method of treating depression. The University of Essex conducted a study with depressed people to test the benefits of a thirty-minute walk in the country compared to a thirty-minute walk around a shopping center. The results were astonishing. Seventy-one percent of the participants felt much better after the walk in the country, and 90 percent said their self-esteem had increased. Forty-five percent of the walkers in the shopping center felt better, but 22 percent said they were more depressed after the walk.[17]

See if you can find a sacred space in your immediate environment. You may have a place in your garden that you might dedicate to this purpose. You might find it in a nearby park or nature reserve. Even if you find it impossible to find somewhere in your neighborhood, you can still create an imaginary sacred space in your mind.

Visit your sacred space as often as you can, if only for your mental health. If you are extremely busy or the weather is bad, you can visit it in your mind. You'll find it highly restorative to close your eyes for a few moments and picture your sacred space.

---

17. Francesca Price, "Natural Progression," *New Zealand Listener*, vol. 208, no. 3499, June 2007 (Auckland, New Zealand: APN Specialist Publications), 36.

I visit my sacred space almost every day. Sometimes I have a specific reason for the visit, but usually I have no specific aim in mind other than to meditate and commune with nature. I look after the area around my sacred space. If I take anything from the area—such as a flower, feather, or stone—I either leave something in its place or I do a small task as a way of giving thanks.

Purification

Native Americans use a number of purifying herbs to cleanse the spirit and relax the mind and body. The three most important are cedar, sage, and sweetgrass.

Cedar

Cedar is a highly effective herb for both physical and spiritual healing. The smoke produced when it is burned has a calming effect that enhances clarity of mind. It also raises the spirit.

Sage

There are five hundred varieties of sage. Sage releases all negativity and has a positive effect on the mind, body, and spirit.

Sweetgrass

Sweetgrass provides strength, guidance, and support. It is often plaited into braids that produce a pleasing sweet-smelling smoke when burned.

Smudging

Smudging is performed to cleanse the aura. It is also performed to cleanse objects, rooms, houses, and sacred places. Smudge sticks can be bought from most New Age stores, and frequently contain sage, cedar, and sweetgrass. When lit, smudge sticks provide a fragrant smoke that can be wafted over people or used to scent and cleanse a particular space. Some people use a fan when smudging people. I prefer to follow the outline of the person's body while thinking of my purpose in performing the smudging.

Although shamanism is thousands of years old, it is still valid today. For instance, shamanism is a highly effective way of becoming aware of the spiritual dimension in nature. It also helps us to realize that we are all interconnected, that we all come from Mother Earth and we all have a duty to look after her. By doing this, and gaining a holistic understanding of the entire universe, we become part of an ancient and timeless spiritual tradition.

One of the duties of a shaman is to provide protection for his or her community. How flowers can be used for this purpose is the subject of the next chapter.

seven

Flowers for Protection

hen I mention psychic protection to people, they usually assume I am referring to methods of warding off a psychic attack directed by one person against another. The methods in this chapter will work for that, but situations of this sort are extremely rare and appear more often in fiction than in everyday life.

Fortunately, few of us are attacked psychically by others, but we all suffer from the stresses, strains, and anxieties of everyday life. Most people can handle these for a period of time, especially when they are in good health, but eventually they can wear down even the most robust of people.

Some people have more delicate constitutions than others, and they are more susceptible to psychic attack. However, everyone opens themselves up to the possibility at different times. Whenever you open your heart to others, for instance, you make yourself vulnerable to attack. I'm not saying you should prevent this from happening by never opening yourself up to others. Of course you should, and you should do it often. However, be aware that the possibility of attack is there whenever you do so.

Psychic attacks usually enter the body through one of the chakras, the seven energy centers found in the etheric body, or aura. Here are two examples. When you open yourself up to others, you open your heart chakra. Whenever you give your personal power to someone else, voluntarily or involuntarily, you open up your solar chakra; a good example might be a parent who is still controlling you, even though you are now an adult.

The chakras are revolving, wheel-like circles of subtle energies that absorb higher energies and make them available to the physical body. They are situated inside the aura alongside the central nervous system. In the East they are usually depicted as lotus flowers, a circle surrounded by petals. The word *chakra* comes from the Sanskrit word for "wheel," as chakras are seen as revolving circles of energy. They play an important role in our physical, mental, and emotional health, as well as our spiritual development. There are seven major chakras, which lie alongside the spinal column, and dozens of minor chakras, which exist throughout the body.

Root chakra

Color: red

Desire: physical contact

The root chakra is situated at the base of the spine and keeps us grounded, making us feel secure and comfortable. It is responsible for self-preservation, physical strength, and also looks after our sense of taste and smell. The Sanskrit word for the root chakra, *muladhara*, means "support." This chakra makes us feel enthusiastic and full of energy. It gives us courage and persistence.

Sacral chakra

Color: orange

Desires: respect and acceptance

The sacral chakra is situated at the level of the sacrum in the small of the back, about two inches below the navel. The sacral chakra is concerned with the fluidic functions of the body; it looks after these functions and is concerned especially with our sexual energy. It is also concerned with creativity and emotional balance. This chakra enables us to relate to other people easily, and provides optimism and hope.

Solar chakra

Color: yellow

Desire: to understand

The solar chakra is situated just above the navel at the level of the solar plexus. The Sanskrit word for this chakra is *manipuraka*, which means "jewel of the navel." This chakra looks after the emotions and provides self-esteem, optimism, warmth, and happiness. It also relates to absorption and digestion of food, which is closely connected to our physical well-being. This chakra is a source of power whenever you are starting a new venture.

Heart chakra

Color: green

Desires: to love and be loved

The heart chakra is found in the center of the chest in line with the heart. It is concerned with love, harmony, understanding, higher consciousness, and the sense of touch. When we are "in touch" with someone, our heart often goes out to them. This chakra enhances compassion and a respect for self and others. When the heart chakra is balanced, the person finds it easy to express emotions.

Throat chakra

Color: blue

Desire: inner peace

The throat chakra is situated at the level of the throat. It relates to creativity, communication, and self-expression. When it is balanced, the throat chakra provides contentment, peace of mind, and a strong faith.

Brow chakra

Color: indigo

Desire: to be in harmony with the universe

The brow chakra is situated in the forehead, between the eyebrows. In Sanskrit, this chakra is called *ajna*, which means "command." This chakra looks after the mind, and in a sense is the command center that controls the other chakras. It is involved with insight and the intellect, as well as psychic perception. This chakra increases our understanding of the everyday world by making us aware that we are essentially spiritual beings experiencing a physical incarnation. This chakra enhances our intuition and enables us to sense other people's feelings and moods.

Crown chakra

Color: violet

Desire: universal understanding

The crown chakra is situated at the very top of the head and is the strongest energy center of the body. Artists sometimes depict this chakra as a halo. The tonsure of monks began as a way of exposing this area. The Sanskrit word for crown chakra is *sahasrara*, which means "thousand." The symbol of this chakra is the thousand-petaled lotus.

This chakra makes us understand the interconnectedness of all living things. It also harmonizes the interior and exterior sides of our natures. It is our connection to the universal life force. When all the chakras are properly balanced, this chakra provides wisdom and enlightenment.

Psychic Protection with Flowers

Whenever you sense you are becoming overwhelmed with stress, worry, anxiety or overtiredness, close your eyes for a few seconds and visualize a rose. The rose is the universal symbol of love, and visualizing it enables your aura to instantly block off any negative energy.

One of my clients is a man in his early fifties. I have known him for more than thirty years, and for many of those years I found myself totally drained of energy after he left. People who have this effect on others are called "psychic vampires." They gain their energy by effectively stealing it from others. Usually this is done unconsciously, but I have met a few people who appear to do it deliberately. Most people have a psychic vampire or two in their lives.

One day I told a friend about the feelings of negativity and overwhelming tiredness I felt whenever this man visited me. This friend suggested I visualize a beautiful rose halfway between my client and me the next time he came for an appointment. I was a little bit skeptical, but when I tried it I found it to be an amazingly simple and effective remedy.

Nowadays, whenever I find myself in the presence of a psychic vampire or anyone who is expressing negative thoughts, I visualize the rose and immediately feel protected and safe. When I do this, none of their negativity is able to reach me.

I have experimented with other flowers, too. All flowers seem to work, but as the rose seems to have more potency and power than any other flower, it is the one I use all the time.

I also experimented with a vase of roses in my office. I looked at the roses whenever I experienced negativity. This worked well, too, but was no better than simply visualizing an imaginary rose. Also, visualization can be done any time, anywhere. It might be a fun image, but it's not practical to carry a bouquet of roses everywhere you go.

Ten Steps to Psychic Protection

Imagining a rose is a highly effective way of warding off an unexpected psychic attack. However, you can strengthen your aura with a brief daily exercise that will provide you with protection from the everyday stresses of life. As you will see, it is best to do this exercise early in the day. I sometimes do it when I first wake up, before getting out of bed.

1. Set aside ten minutes of time every day for contemplation.

2. Sit in a recliner-type chair and make yourself as comfortable as possible. Close your eyes. Relax your mind and body by taking several slow, deep breaths. Consciously relax the muscles in the toes of each foot. Once you feel they are relaxed, focus on your feet. As each part of your body relaxes, gradually work your way up to the top of your head until your entire body is completely relaxed.

3. Imagine you are in a beautiful garden. It is late spring or early summer, and you're enjoying a perfect day. It's pleasantly

warm, with just the merest hint of a cooling breeze. The garden is full of the most magnificent flowers you have ever seen. In your mind, walk around the garden, pausing every now and again to look, touch, and smell certain flowers.

4. Walk around the garden for as long as you wish. You have all the time in the world, and you are completely alone in this magnificent garden. You remember that you are allowed to take one flower with you when you leave.

5. Walk around the garden again, but this time search for the one flower that holds the most meaning to you today. The choice might be obvious, or you might have to select between a number of possibilities.

6. When you find your flower, ask it for its permission for you to pick it and take it with you. Once you sense the flower's assent, thank it and then pick the flower.

7. Visualize yourself leaving the garden with the flower and going through the routine of a normal day. Notice the subtle changes the flower brings to everything you're doing. Feel the calmness inside you, no matter what is occurring in the everyday world.

8. Take a slow, deep breath. Mentally count from one to five, and open your eyes. Do not get up immediately. Allow a minute or two to think about your guided visualization.

9. Get up and carry on with your day. Imagine the flower you chose is with you throughout the day.

10. When you get to bed at night, think about the day you have just had. Ask yourself what effect, if any, the imaginary flower you chose had on your day. Allow yourself to drift off to sleep, knowing that you'll be able to visit the magnificent garden again tomorrow and choose another flower. Of course, you can always choose the same flower again if you wish.

I find that this is a particularly useful meditation. I enjoy choosing different flowers and noticing the effects each one has on me during the day. Sometimes I choose the same flower for days on end. This might be because the energies are too subtle for me to pick them up in one day. Just as often, it might be because the energies are so profound that I want to experience them again and again.

Each time you perform this meditation, you are strengthening your aura, making you more and more immune to psychic attack.

Protecting Your Home Environment

Rose water is an effective way to protect yourself and your home. You can buy rose water at many drugstores, but I usually prefer to make my own. Here are two different ways of doing so:

Method One

Place a teaspoon of rose petals into a cup of boiling water. Allow it to steep for about fifteen minutes. Add a quarter of a cup of alcohol and stir the mixture for thirty seconds. Allow it to cool before use. I normally use vodka for the alcohol, as it is an extremely good preservative.

Method Two

Prepare a solution of alcohol and water. It should be approximately 75 percent water and 25 percent alcohol. Add a few drops of rose essential oil to this solution. Stir and smell the fragrance. Add more drops of essential oil if you prefer a stronger scent. It is important to use genuine rose oil rather than synthetic substitutes.

How to Use Rose Water

Start by facing south and blessing your rose water. South is the direction of Michael, the archangel of courage and strength. Dip a finger into the rose water and anoint yourself on each of your chakras.

Once you have done that, you can use the rose water to trace the frames of the windows and doors in your home. I like to work around the house in a clockwise direction and trace the frames in the same direction. However, this is a personal choice and you may prefer to work differently.

An acquaintance of mine puts her rose water in a spray bottle. Doing this means she can spray any area she wishes quickly and easily. She uses it both indoors and out to provide protection for herself. She also frequently sprays any areas that seem to possess negative energy.

Bach Flowers for Protection

The Bach flower remedies that we looked at in chapter 4 can also be used for personal protection. Centauria, cherry plum, gentian, gorse, larch, red chestnut, rockrose, scleranthus, sweet chestnut, and wild oat are all good remedies that can be used for protection. Dr. Bach's Rescue Remedy (rockrose, star of Bethlehem, impatiens, plum, and clematis) is also extremely good for personal protection.

Place three drops of your chosen remedy under your tongue three times a day whenever you need protection. You can take more drops, if necessary, but three drops three times a day is sufficient for almost every eventuality.

Our forebears used flowers for many purposes in addition to protection. One of the most intriguing uses they were put to became hugely popular in the nineteenth century—this was the language of flowers, which we'll discuss in the next chapter.

eight

The Language
of Flowers

*F*lowers have always possessed hidden meanings. There is evidence that the Chinese practiced the language of flowers five thousand years ago.[18] The ancient Egyptians used it, too, associating the lotus with beauty and divinity, and the iris with power. The Greeks had many propitious flowers, which they formed into garlands and wreaths to crown their heroes. During the Crusades, the wives of soldiers created embroideries that included borage, which signified courage.

William Shakespeare had a vast knowledge of flower meanings. His audiences did, too. In *Hamlet* (1601), Ophelia says:

> There's rosemary, that's for remembrance; pray you, love, remember. And there is pansies, that's for thoughts. There's fennel for you [flattery], and columbines [folly]. There's rue for you [contrition]; and here's some for me. We may call it herb of grace a Sundays. O, you must wear your rue with a difference. There's a daisy [innocence]; I would give you some violets [blue violets = loyalty; white violets = innocence], but they wither'd all when my father died.
>
> —*Hamlet*, act 4, scene 5

In *The Winter's Tale* (1610–1611), Shakespeare has Perdita offer some visitors a selection of winter herbs:

> Reverend sirs,
> For you there's rosemary and rue; these keep
> Seeming, and savour, all the winter long:
> Grace and remembrance, be to you both,
> And welcome to our shearing!
>
> (act 4, scene 4)

Her visitors comment on her choice, taking it as a charming reference to their mature years. Perdita replies that it's the middle of

---

18. Olive Dunn, *Delights of Floral Language* (Auckland, New Zealand: Random House New Zealand, 1993), 8.

summer and her favorite spring flowers had gone. The only flowers are "our carnations and streak'd gillyvors, which some call nature's bastards." She then offers a more appropriate bouquet:

> Here's flowers for you;
> Hot lavender, mints, savory, marjoram;
> The marigold, that goes to bed wi' the sun
> And with him rises weeping: these are flowers
> Of middle summer, and I think they are given
> To men of middle age. You're very welcome.

(act 4, scene 4)

Shakespeare mentioned many flowers in his plays, but his favorite seems to have been the rose, which he referred to at least sixty times.

The language of flowers was introduced to the West by Lady Mary Wortley Montagu (1689–1762), an English poet and early feminist who was married to the British ambassador to the Porte of Constantinople. While living in Turkey, Lady Mary became fascinated with the Turkish *selam*, or language of objects. This was a secret, symbolic language that used objects, mainly flowers, to deliver a coded message that only the recipient could understand. An iris, for example, meant *no*, but a grape hyacinth meant *yes*.

This secret language became extremely popular in France, possibly because both Marie Antoinette and Josephine adored flowers. The first book on the subject, *Sur le Langage des Fleurs* by Joseph Hammer-Purgstall, was published in 1809. The most famous book on the subject, *Le Langage des Fleurs* by Madame Charlotte de la Tour, was published in 1819 and became an instant bestseller. It was translated into most European languages and formed the basis of dozens of copycat books. The first British book on the subject was *Flora Domestica, or The Portable Flower-Garden* by Elizabeth Kent. It was published in 1823. Nine years later, in 1832, the first American book on the subject was published. This was *Flora's Dictionary* by Mrs. Elizabeth Washington Gamble Wirt (1784–1857). Between

1800 and 1937, fifty-seven writers produced ninety-eight books on the language of flowers.[19]

The incredible popularity of the language of flowers might seem strange today, but in the nineteenth century it was considered good etiquette to give and receive bouquets of flowers. Men gave them to their sweethearts, and women gave them to female friends and children. A man who found it impossible to write a love letter or poem could create a bouquet of flowers that conveyed his feelings. However, he had to be careful, as it was easy to accidentally send the wrong message. There were, for instance, at least thirty potential meanings for roses. In addition, the recipient had to recognize the flowers. This was not always easy, as flowers sometimes had several different names. One way of overcoming potential problems was to include a list of the flowers, along with their intended meanings.

At times the different books on the subject contradicted themselves, but here is a list of the most common meanings:

Acacia (white): pure love, friendship. "I idolize you."

Agapanthus: love letter. "I love you more than words can say."

Agrimony: gratitude. "Please accept my grateful thanks."

Amaryllis: beauty, pride, haughtiness. "You are untouchable."

Anemone: truth, sincerity. "I put all my faith in you."

Angelica: inspiration. "My love for you is all the inspiration I need."

Apple blossom: beauty, goodness, and temptation. "You can lead me anywhere you wish."

Arum: aspiration. "Our love will continue to grow."

Aster: afterthoughts. "I regret my impulsiveness."

Azalea: happiness, love, and romance. "You have captured my heart."

Basil: formal best wishes. "I enjoyed our conversation."

Bay: unchanging affection. "Only death could change me."

---

19. Olive Dunn, *Delights of Floral Language* (Auckland, New Zealand: Random House New Zealand, 1993), 8.

Begonia: unrequited love, warning. "We are being watched."

Bellflower (campanula): gratitude. "I appreciate everything about you."

Bergamot: attraction. "You are irresistible."

Bindweed: humility. "Please forgive me."

Bird of paradise: magnificence. "I am in awe of your beauty, personality, and temperament."

Blackberry: pride. "Your haughtiness does not become you."

Bluebell: constancy, faithfulness, and fidelity. "I am true to you and only you."

Borage: dismissive. "Your attentions are not welcome."

Box: stoicism. "Neither cold nor heat, shade nor sunlight, nor anything else can change my love."

Bracken: enchantment. "You fascinate me."

Bramble: remorse. "Please forgive me."

Broom: ardor. "The yellow of these flowers provide a mere hint of the strength of my love."

Buttercup: radiance and cheerfulness. (Buttercup is sometimes used to gently mock someone.) "Your golden beauty dazzles me."

Camellia: attractiveness. "How beautiful you look today."

Carnation, pink: encouragement. "I hope to see you again soon."

Carnation, red: passionate love. "My heart longs for you."

Carnation, white: platonic love. "I offer you a chaste and pure love."

Carnation, yellow: admiration. "I have long worshipped you from afar."

Chamomile: fortitude and persistence. "I admire your courage and strength of character."

Cherry blossom: growth. "To the development of our friendship."

Chrysanthemum, bronze: friendship. "I value your friendship, but I do not love you."

Chrysanthemum, red: reciprocated love. "I love you."

Chrysanthemum, yellow: jilted love. "My heart belongs to someone else."

Chrysanthemum, white: truth and honesty. "I believe in you."

Cineraria: joy and delight. "Your company is delightful."

Cinquefoil: beloved child. "My love for you is chaste and pure."

Citron: communication. "I will write to you every day."

Clematis: appreciation of a good intellect. "I appreciate your beautiful mind."

Clover, four leaf: adoration. "Be mine!"

Clover, three leaf: the Trinity. "God favors us."

Clover, white: promise. "I will be true."

Columbine, purple: resolve, steadfastness. "I will never give up on you."

Columbine, white: foolishness. "You are foolish to continue pursuing me."

Convolvulus: separation. "I will miss you terribly."

Coriander: hidden depths. "Do not judge me on appearances."

Cornflower: delicacy. "You are graceful and refined."

Cowslip: beauty and grace. "You are delightful."

Crocus: fondness. "I cherish the thought of you."

Cyclamen: indifference. "I feel nothing for you."

Daffodil: respect and regard. "I admire you greatly."

Dahlia, red: rebuff. "Our paths will not cross again."

Dahlia, white: dismissal. "Goodbye."

Dahlia, yellow: distaste. "You do not appeal to me."

Daisy: innocence, delay. "I will let you know in a day or two."

Dandelion: absurdity. "You are too pretentious to take seriously."

Daphne: worship. "I exist solely to please you."

Deadly nightshade: deception. "I do not trust you."

Dianthus: need. "Please come quickly."

Digitalis: delay. "I'll be with you as soon as I can."

Evening primrose: inconstancy. "We cannot go on like this."

Fern: domestic happiness. "My home is your home."

Feverfew: protection, warmth. "Let me look after you."

Forget-me-not: remembrance. "Please think of me while I'm away."

Forsythia: anticipation. "I await your return."

Foxglove: insincerity, shallowness. "I doubt you really love me."

Fuchsia: warning. "Be careful. Your lover is false."

Gardenia: sweetness. "You are as perfect as this flower."

Gentian: sadness. "How could you treat me this way?"

Geranium, pink: doubt. "Kindly explain yourself."

Geranium, scarlet: duplicity. "I do not trust you."

Geranium, white: indecision. "I have not yet decided."

Gladiolus: pain. "Your words have cut me to the quick."

Hawthorn: hope. "Despite your remarks, I will continue to earn your love."

Heather: solitude, protection. "I can't wait for you to return."

Heliotrope: devotion. "You are the sun in my life."

Hellebore: scandal. "Speak to no one of our love."

Hemlock: scandal. "I have been unjustly condemned."

Hibiscus: delicate beauty. "You are perfection."

Holly: domestic happiness. "We possess riches beyond compare."

Hollyhock: simplicity. "All we need is our love."

Honeysuckle: plighted troth. "This is but a small token of my love."

Hyacinth, blue: devotion. "I am your humble and devoted servant."

Hyacinth, white: admiration. "I admire and respect you."

Hydrangea: fickleness, heartlessness. "Why aren't you constant?"

Hyssop: stirring of the heart. "Why does my heart light up whenever you appear?"

Iris: ardor. "I adore you."

Ivy: attachment. "Be mine forever."

Jasmine: eloquence. "I love your heart, mind, and soul."

Jonquil: appeal. "Do I have any chance with you?"

Laburnum: neglect. "Why do you ignore me?"

Larkspur: thoughtlessness and carelessness. "Please forgive me."

Laurel: honor. "I am so proud of you."

Lavender: distrust. "I'm not sure I believe you."

Lilac, purple: first love. "I have never loved another."

Lilac, white: innocence. "I adore your youth, beauty, and integrity."

Lily, white: purity and modesty. "May I kiss your hand?"

Lily-of-the-valley: return of happiness. "I worship you."

London pride: flirtation. "Let's spend time together soon."

Lotus flower: estrangement. "Can we not get together again?"

Lupin: over-boldness. "The more haste, the less speed."

Magnolia: fortitude. "I will wait for you."

Maiden-hair: discretion. "You can rely on my word of honor."

Marigold: despair. "Will I never see you again?"

Marjoram: modesty. "Your forwardness makes me blush."

Mimosa: sensitivity. "You are too forward."

Mistletoe: kisses. "I send you thousands of kisses."

Morning glory: affectation. "Please be yourself. The real you enchants me."

Mulberry: prudence. "One step at a time, my love."

Myrtle: love and protection. "You are mine and I am yours."

Narcissus: self-love. "You love only yourself."

Nasturtium: artifice. "I love you just the way you are."

Oleander: let down. "A false friend has betrayed us."

Olive: peace. "Let us be friends."

Orange blossom: purity. "My virginity is precious to me."

Orchid: luxury, love, and refinement. "I will tend to your every need."

Pansy, purple: think of me. "You occupy my thoughts."

Pansy, white: loving thoughts. "You are always on my mind."

Pansy, yellow: remembrance. "I'll always cherish our time together."

Peony: regrets, contrition. "I beg your forgiveness."

Periwinkle, blue: early friendship. "I cherish the memory of the day we met."

Petunia: closeness. "I love being near to you."

Phlox: flame of love. "My heart burns for you."

Poinsettia: positivity. "Be of good cheer, my love."

Polyanthus: confidence. "Until death do us part."

Poppy: consolation. "Please accept my deepest condolences."

Poppy, red: remembrance. "We will remember him/her."

Primrose: start of love. "My feelings for you are growing day by day."

Rhododendron: abundance and pride. "I can give you all that life has to offer."

Rose, red: love, passion. "I love you."

Rose, white: silence. "Our love must remain secret."

Rose, pink: grace and beauty. "I admire you."

Rosemary: remembrance. "I will never forget you."

Sage: good health, longevity. "Our love will last for all eternity."

Snapdragon: refusal. "You mean nothing to me."

Snowdrop: consolation, hope. "I'll continue trying to gain your heart."

Star of Bethlehem: reconciliation. "Our love will blossom and grow day by day."

Sunflower: loyalty, haughtiness, and ostentation. "Baubles of gold do not impress me."

Sweet pea: departure. "I'll think of you all day, every day."

Thyme: domesticity. "You'd make a good wife and mother."

Tulip, red: announcement of love. "I want to tell the world about you."

Tulip, yellow: unrequited love. "I still adore you."

Verbena: enchantment. "You have cast a spell on me."

Violet: faithfulness and modesty. "I will always be true to you."

Wallflower: fidelity and constancy. "I am true to you, my love."

Water–lily: coldness. "I wish you luck elsewhere."
Yew: tears. "My tears will cease when I'm in your arms again."
Zinnia: inconstancy. "Goodbye. You are too fickle for me."

The Lovers' Clock

When lovers needed a secret method of arranging times to meet, they used twelve flowers to indicate the twelve hours. Even today some people create in their gardens an attractive floral clock that has each flower in the correct position. The flowers are:

1 o'clock: rosemary

2 o'clock: marjoram

3 o'clock: violet

4 o'clock: jonquil

5 o'clock: sweet pea

6 o'clock: herb Robert

7 o'clock: tulip

8 o'clock: bluebell

9 o'clock: primrose

10 o'clock: clove pink

11 o'clock: sweet sultan

12 o'clock: carnation

Tussie-mussies

Tussie-mussies are circular nosegays or posies of flowers that are made to convey a message using the language of flowers. The term first appeared in print as *tuzzy mussy* in 1440. *Tussie* probably comes from the word *tussock*, while *mussie* was the damp moss that was pressed around the stems of the flowers to keep them moist.[20]

In seventeenth-century England, small bouquets or posies of herbs were used to protect people from the plague, as the old nursery rhyme attests:

---

20. *Tussie-Mussies: The Victorian Art of Expressing Yourself in the Language of Flowers* by Geraldine Adamich Laufer (New York: Workman, 1993), 12.

Ring-a-ring o' roses,
A pocket full of posies,
A-tishoo! A-tishoo!
We all fall down.

From the sixteenth to the nineteenth centuries, tussie-mussies were considered essential adornments and were carried, worn in the hair, and pinned to clothes and hats. Most of the time, these tussie-mussies were made from fragrant herbs such as chamomile, hyssop, lavender, marjoram, rosemary, rue, sage, and thyme. Until Victorian times, tussie-mussies were simply small bouquets of attractive flowers and conveyed no message other than affection. However, in the prim and proper Victorian society, they provided a perfect way of exchanging secret messages. Some of these messages were extremely complex. A bouquet containing agapanthus, anemone, bergamot, red and pink carnations, and red roses conveys a totally different message from a bouquet containing amaryllis, blackberry, cyclamen, red dahlias, and narcissus.

An admirer would wait anxiously to see what the object of their affections did with their tussie-mussies. It was a sign of caution if a woman wore it in her hair. It indicated friendship if she placed it in her cleavage. The admirers all hoped to find it over her heart, as this was a sign of love.

Tussie-mussies are not hard to make. Once you have selected the flowers, you should strip off any surplus leaves, cut the stems at an angle, and place the flowers in water for an hour or two. I use lukewarm water rather than cold water. Choose a flower to go in the center of the tussie-mussie. A rosebud, or any flower that is slightly larger than the others, works well. Surround this first flower with a circle of smaller flowers. Continue adding different flowers in concentric circles. Bind the stalks together with twine or a rubber band as you work. Surround the finished posy with leaves or other foliage and then cover the stalks with waxed paper.

The final step is to tie an attractive ribbon around the paper to hold everything in place.

• • •

The language of flowers played an extremely useful role in Victorian society, as it enabled effective secret communication between people, especially people in love. Often, these people also wanted a glimpse into the future to see if their relationship would develop and endure. Consequently, they engaged in flower divination, which we will look at in the next chapter.

nine

Flower Divination

ivination is the art and practice of predicting the future. Since the beginning of time, people have had a strong desire to part the veil and gain insight into what lies ahead. Most people want to know what the future holds for them.

Floramancy, the art of divining with flowers, was popular in ancient Greece and is still practiced today. The art is based on the belief that flowers are especially sensitive and pick up vibrations and energies from their environment. Consequently, they can be used to clarify ongoing situations and reveal the future.

There is a great deal of evidence that flowers are extremely sensitive and respond to their environment. By inventing instruments to detect the minute responses plants make to external stimuli, Sir Jagadis Bose (1858–1937), an Indian physicist and plant physiologist, demonstrated that plants have feelings. Bose also discovered that plants grow faster when exposed to pleasant music.

Luther Burbank (1849–1926), the American botanist and horticulturist, proved that plants have a central nervous system and respond to words, attention, and love. He believed this is why some people have "green fingers" and can make anything grow, while other people find it hard to grow anything. March 7th, Burbank's birthday, is Arbor Day in California, and every year on this day trees are planted in his memory.

In 1972, Dr. V. Pushkin, a Russian scientist, proved that plants have emotions. He attached an encephalograph to a geranium leaf to record how it reacted when kind and unkind words were said to it. The plant responded in exactly the same way a person would.

In 1966, Cleve Backster, an American polygraph scientist, discovered he could measure the changes in electrical resistance when a plant was harmed or threatened. He attached a plant to a polygraph machine and mentally threatened it. To his surprise, the plant responded. Further research demonstrated that plants respond to a wide range of emotions and thoughts.[21]

Divination makes it sound as if our lives are predetermined. Fortunately, this is not the case. We all possess free will. A fortune-teller may see, for example, a new love entering your life three months from now. If you decide to spend every night at home on your own watching television, this prediction is unlikely to come true. You have to act to make things happen.

Almost everyone has practiced a form of flower divination. I vividly remember, as a child, blowing the seeds off a dandelion and chanting, "She loves me, she loves me not."

A lady I met in Wiltshire used onions to determine the outcome of different events. Whenever she had a problem with several possible outcomes, she would write each outcome on pieces of paper and attach each one to a different onion. The onions would be placed side by side and checked on every now and again. The first onion to sprout provided the answer. Many years later, I learned that divination with onions is extremely old. In his book *Anatomy of Melancholy* (1621), Robert Burton (1577–1640) refers to "Cromnysmantia," which is "a kind of Divination with *Onions*, laid on the Altar at Christmas Eve, practiced by Girls, to know they shall be married and how many husbands they shall have." One hundred and fifty years later, John Brand (1744–1806) wrote in his book *Observations on Popular Antiquities* (1777):

> In these same Dayes young wanton Gyrles, that meete
> for Marriage bee, Doe search to know that Names of
> them that shall their husbandes bee. *Four Onyons, five or
> eight, they take, and make in every one Such names* as they
> do fansie most, and best do think upon. Then neere the

---

21. Peter Tompkins and Christopher Bird, *The Secret Life of Plants* (New York: Harper Collins, 1973). See also: Cleve Backster and Flora Powers, *Primary Perception: Biocommunication with Plants, Living Foods, and Human Cells* (Anza, CA: White Rose Millennium Press, 2003).

chimney them they set and that same *onyon* then That
first doth sproute doth surely bear the name of their
good man.

The author of the medieval song "Scarborough Fair" is unknown.
Because it was sung by numerous troubadours and not written
down for many years, there are many different versions of the song.
"Scarborough Fair" recalls four divination plants that originally
brought the singer and his lover together:

> Where are you going? To Scarborough Fair?
> Parsley, sage, rosemary, and thyme,
> Remember me to a bonny lass there,
> For once she was a true lover of mine.

The following verses describe a succession of impossible activities
she would need to accomplish to regain his love:

> Tell her to make me a cambric shirt,
> Parsley, sage, rosemary, thyme,
> Without any needle or thread work'd in't,
> And she shall be a true love of mine.

The meanings of the four herbs are unknown to most people
who listen to this song today. In medieval times, parsley was eaten
at meals to take away any bitter taste and to aid digestion. Sage
has always symbolized strength. Rosemary symbolizes faithfulness, remembrance, and feminine love. Thyme symbolizes courage.
Ladies embroidered images of thyme for knights to place in their
shields to give them courage when going into battle. Consequently,
the herbs might also convey a secret message from the jilted singer.

Divination with Parsley, Sage, Rosemary, and Thyme

An interesting divination can be performed with finely chopped
herbs. Parsley, sage, rosemary, and thyme are the herbs most usually associated with divination. Consequently, use them if possible,
although you can substitute other herbs if necessary. It is better

to use freshly chopped herbs, but you can use dried herbs if no fresh herbs are available. Think of a question or concern. Mix the chopped herbs together and scatter them on to a large piece of white paper. Ideally, the paper should be rough rather than smooth. For that reason, inexpensive paper is usually better for this divination than more expensive paper. You may see a picture or pattern that creates thoughts in your mind right away. If this does not happen, hold the paper by each end and gently shake it to create a different arrangement of herbs. Continue doing this until the herbs create a formation that relates to your concern. Gaze at this pattern and see what thoughts come into your mind. If you need more clarification, shake the paper again until another pattern emerges. You can do this several times, if necessary, until you have a clear picture of the outcome of your concern.

My first experience of flower divination occurred in a Spiritualist church I visited as a teenager. The medium who conducted the service passed around a large basket of freshly cut flowers, and everyone in the congregation chose one. She then walked around the room giving brief psychometry readings to people based on the flowers they had chosen. Psychometry is the art of receiving feelings and intuitive insights about someone by holding something they have been in contact with. Usually, this is an object they have owned for some time, but plants accept psychic impressions almost instantly, which can be read and interpreted by competent psychometrists.

An interesting form of long-term flower divination is practiced in the Far East. Three carnations on a single stem are placed in the hair of a teenager and observed until the flowers start wilting. If the uppermost flower dies first, it is a sign that the teenager's later years will be the most difficult. The middle years will be the most difficult if the middle flower dies first, and the early years will be the hardest if the bottom flower dies first. If the flowers take a long time to die, the person will lead a successful and happy life.

You can find out what sort of year you can expect by noting the day on which you see the first flower of spring:

Sunday: a year of unexpected delights and good fortune
Monday: good luck all year
Tuesday: a successful year as long as you apply yourself
Wednesday: you, or someone close to you, will get married
Thursday: a happy year but one with only modest financial success
Friday: hard work pays off handsomely
Saturday: good luck passes you by

Flower Reading for Yourself

Until you learn something about the art of flower reading, it is easy to choose a flower that appeals to you. Once you have learned something about the art, it becomes more difficult because you are able to interpret the different shapes and colors of different flowers. However, even experts are still able to choose a suitable flower. Instead of choosing a flower solely on its aesthetic appeal, you can allow yourself to be intuitively led to the flower that is most important to you at that time. You will sometimes be surprised when you let your intuition choose a flower for you, but it will always be the flower you need.

Once you start choosing a flower for yourself on a regular basis, you will find that you do not necessarily have to pick it. You can admire the flower, interpret it, thank it, and leave it on the plant—unless you want to carry it with you for some reason.

Flower Reading for Others

Most people have never met a flower reader. Once you develop your skills at reading flowers you will find yourself in great demand. The best places to practice are parks and gardens where there are a wide variety of flowers on display. Ask your friends to choose a single flower, which you then interpret for them.

Another alternative is to have a vase containing a wide selection of different flowers. Have as many different colors and types of flowers as possible. Your friends can select a single flower from the selection available. This is the method I use when doing flower readings in public.

Yet another possibility is to have a large selection of photographs of different flowers. Most of mine have been clipped from gardening magazines. I pasted them onto sheets of 8½" x 11" cards and laminated them for protection. Recently I created another, smaller set of flower photographs that I glued to index cards. I can carry these in a pocket. They are good in impromptu situations if the subject of flower reading happens to come up. They are also more convenient to carry than the larger photographs. I also have several books on flowers that are full of color illustrations. People can browse through these and select any flower that appeals to them. The advantage of these possibilities is that you can offer an almost unlimited range of flowers to choose from. The disadvantage is that you cannot hold or smell the flower.

I have another method that I use if none of the other alternatives are available. I hand the client a pad of paper and a set of colored pencils and ask them to draw a flower. This can be extremely revealing as the color choices reflect the person's innermost feelings at the time they drew the flower.

Flower Reading 101

The reading is based on several different aspects of the flower. These are:

> **Theme of the flower:** Obviously, if you know something about the traditional meanings of the flower, these will come into your interpretation. Someone choosing a red rose, for instance, is more likely to be thinking of love than about their mortgage.

Shape: Flowers come in all sorts of shapes and sizes. Fortunately, the shapes can be classified under several headings, and these are interpreted.

Color: Every color has a meaning that plays an important part in flower interpretation.

Number of petals: Basic numerology plays a role in flower reading and is used to interpret the number of petals on the chosen flower.

Aroma: Different scents can also be interpreted, and these provide additional insight into the reading.

Stalk: The stalk can be divided into three equal parts. The third closest to the flower relates to the future, while the middle section relates to the present and the bottom third relates to the past.

Theme of the Flower

This is not always apparent but when it is, it gives you a vital clue as to what the person you are reading for is thinking about.

Cleansing is the theme of the primrose family. People who choose primrose are reevaluating their path in life and are searching for a more positive future.

Communication and courage are the themes of the snapdragon family. People who choose snapdragons tend to keep their feelings secret and find it hard to speak openly.

Confidence, self-esteem, and security are the themes of the bluebell family. People who choose bluebells relate well with others.

Energy is the theme of the mint family. People who choose mint are suffering from mental or physical exhaustion. This flower can help them gain new energy.

Grace and potential are the themes of the orchid family. The Greeks and Romans associated orchids with love, which is why they are dedicated to Venus. People who choose orchids are seeking universal love and understanding.

Healing is the theme of the parsley family. People who choose parsley are seeking healing, especially emotional healing.

Hope and happy anticipation are the themes of snowdrops and daffodils. These are the first flowers to appear in spring, and for that reason they symbolize new life.

Innocence is the theme of the daisy family. Children have always loved daisies, which is why daisies have become associated with innocence. People who choose daisies are looking for patience and strength when facing a difficult situation.

Inspiration is the theme of the iris family. This is because irises have traditionally been associated with the rainbow. Irises enable great thoughts (inspiration) that can then be put into practice to obtain worthwhile results.

Love is the theme for the rose family. The color of the rose provides further insights. A red rose indicates passion, while a white rose is virginal, platonic, or idealistic.

Peace and purity are the themes of the lily family. Your questioner is likely to have a question involving nurturing, calm, or any other traditionally feminine quality.

Purification is the theme of the eucalyptus family. People who choose eucalyptus are seeking to let go of the past and start anew.

Sensitivity is the theme of the violet family. People who choose violets are seeking psychic healing and protection. They often need help in standing up and asserting themselves.

Sexual problems are the theme of the arum family. People who choose arum are facing difficulties and need to make decisions about this area of their lives.

Stress is the theme of the valerian family. People who choose these flowers are suffering from a variety of stresses in their lives. Valerian can help them realize what these stresses are, and to make any necessary changes in their lives.

Wisdom is the theme of the jasmine family. People who choose jasmine are seeking knowledge and spiritual growth.

Shape

The shape of the chosen flower reveals the person's emotional state. There are nine possibilities:

Bell

Bell-shaped flowers point downward to the ground, showing that people who choose it need grounding. These people find it hard to express their innermost feelings and subconsciously sabotage themselves at a deep, inner level. Choosing a bell-shaped flower helps these people release the blocks that are holding them back, so that they can start fulfilling their hopes and dreams.

Fuchsias and bluebells are good examples of bell-shaped flowers.

Cup

Cup-shaped flowers point upward, revealing the nurturing and caring properties that are associated with them. People who choose cup-shaped flowers feel lacking in love and support from others. Choosing this flower helps them realize their true worth; discovering this helps them to raise their self-esteem.

Good examples of cup-shaped flowers include evening primrose, tulips, and protea.

Jester's hat

The jester's hat is a crescent-shaped flower. It is similar to the bell and cup-shaped flowers but with petals that curl back, making it resemble a jester's hat. People who choose these flowers repress their emotions and find it hard to express their innermost feelings.

Good examples of jester's hat flowers include the nasturtium and tiger lily.

Trumpet

Trumpet-shaped flowers relate to self-expression. People who choose a trumpet-shaped flower need to express themselves in some way—creatively, ideally. They also need to learn to express their true feelings instead of engaging in superficial thoughts and idle conversation for the sake of talking.

Good examples of trumpet-shaped flowers include angel's trumpet, daffodils, and morning glory.

Flame

Flowers that look like a flame are related to the fire element. They give energy and enthusiasm but also show something has to be eliminated (in a sense, burned) or left behind in order for the person to progress. People who choose flame-shaped flowers are seeking new opportunities and a new approach to life.

Good examples of a flame-shaped flower include mullein and red-hot pokers.

Star

Star-shaped flowers have five or six petals that radiate outward. People who choose this shape have a desire for spiritual growth. They are likely to be overly sensitive and suffering from exhaustion or fears that are holding them back.

Borage, iris, and St. John's wort are good examples of star-shaped flowers.

Sun

Flowers containing radiating petals look like popular images of the sun. They usually grow singly on a stem. Because of this, they relate to confidence and self-expression. People who choose sun-like flowers need to learn to accept their personal power, become less serious, and be willing to express themselves openly.

Good examples of sun-like flowers include chrysanthemums, daisies, marigolds, sunflowers, and zinnias.

Drooping spray

Drooping sprays are rows of flowers that grow along an arching branch. Sprays of this sort sway in the breeze, giving an indication of what people who choose them should do. People who choose drooping sprays are often rigid, fixed in outlook, and overwhelmed with responsibilities. Choosing this flower helps them release some of this and "go with the flow."

Good examples of drooping sprays include the scotch broom, willow, and wisteria.

Spike

Spike-like flowers are similar to drooping sprays. However, they point up to the sky rather than drooping downward. Because of this, they symbolize people who are seeking fulfillment and spiritual growth. People who choose spike-like flowers are inclined to be self-critical and feel their best is never good enough. Choosing this flower helps them gain the strength they need to ignore criticism and find their true path in life.

Good examples of spike-like flowers include aloe, lavender, and sage.

Parasol

Parasol flowers are formed when a number of flower stalks, nearly equal in length, spread from a common center. This looks like a parasol or inverted triangle. People who choose a parasol are open, trusting, and intuitive people who are easily hurt. They need to learn to look after themselves rather than to constantly focus on the needs of others.

Good examples of parasol flowers include angelica, feverfew, garlic, and yarrow.

Fountain

Fountain flowers have petals that radiate out from the center in a series of layers. This makes them look similar to a fountain that cascades water in all directions. These flowers appeal to people who are friendly, open-minded, loving, and curious. Such people are also frequently cautious and shy.

Good examples of fountain flowers are camellias, hibiscus, peonies, ranunculus, and zinnias.

Other

Flowers come in all sorts of shapes and forms. Every now and again you'll come across a flower that does not fit easily into the nine other possibilities. People who choose these flowers are seeking emotional freedom and spiritual growth. The Chinese lantern, columbine, and honeysuckle are good examples of flowers in this category.

Color

Flowers come in an enormous range of beautiful colors. People are often attracted to a particular flower because of its color, and these choices can be interpreted. The color chosen determines the qualities the person needs at the time.

Many flowers contain more than one color. The main color of the petals reveals the natural abilities of your client. A different color in the center of the flower reveals the person's innermost nature. The color of the pistils, the seed-bearing organ of the flower, reveals the person's drive and energy. Any additional colors add to, and modify, the basic interpretation of the color of the petals.

Red

Red is a passionate color. Those who like red are independent, enthusiastic, energetic, and passionate people who love life. They are "red-blooded." Red relates to the physical aspects of love. Shakespeare wrote, "My love is like a red, red rose." People who choose red flowers are looking for all the above qualities. They are also looking for motivation and willpower, and the ability to stand up for themselves when necessary.

Pink

Pink is a positive, cheerful, nurturing, and loving color. It relates to innocence and femininity. Pink is calming and encourages positive thoughts about the future. People who choose pink flowers want to love and accept themselves. They desire more love in their lives. This can be—but usually is not—passionate, physical love. These people are often lonely and crave friendship.

Orange and gold

Orange and gold are exciting, stimulating, and joyful colors. They are less forceful than red, since they possess a degree of lightness and forethought. Orange and gold symbolize warmth, tolerance, prosperity, and universal love. In the past, flowers of these colors were used to relieve depression. People who choose orange and gold flowers are seeking the above qualities. They want to be more sociable and positive, and are often wanting to bounce back after a disappointment or heartache.

Yellow

Yellow is lighthearted, carefree, and fun-loving. It is cheerful, positive, and quick-thinking. It relates to verbal communication and creativity. People who choose yellow flowers want to be cheerful and expansive. They also want to communicate and interact well with others.

Green

Green is soothing, restful, and nurturing. It is the color of nature and is highly effective at restoring mind, body, and spirit. It relates to renewal and hope for the future. It symbolizes stability, peace, empathy, and healing. Green flowers are relatively unusual and are most frequently found on grasses. People who choose green flowers want to gain understanding, tolerance, contentment, and emotional stability.

Blue

Blue is the coolest color and has a calming effect on the mind, body, and spirit. Blue symbolizes honesty, sincerity, self-expression, loyalty, tranquility, and stability. People who choose blue flowers are seeking the above qualities. They also want to develop more faith in themselves.

Indigo

Indigo is calm, dignified, idealistic, and caring. It relates to idealism, wisdom, and spirituality. People who choose indigo flowers desire the above qualities and are searching for a spiritual path that will be right for them. They are also seeking confidence, security, and inner peace.

Violet

Violet has always been associated with spirituality. The Greek priests at Eleusis wore violet robes. Violet symbolizes inspiration, spirituality, and the sacred. It stimulates the imagination and enhances intuition. People who choose violet or purple flowers will be going through a stage of transformation, and they desire the above qualities. They may also be suffering from stress, as violet is a gentle, healing color that calms the mind and emotions.

White

White relates to purity, innocence, and forgiveness. It eliminates negativity and fills the mind with feelings of freedom, hope, and endless opportunities. People who choose white (or violet) flowers are undergoing transformation in their lives.

Black

Black relates to sophistication, mystery, and power. People who choose black often have something to hide or are unwilling to reveal too much about themselves. Although it is an unusual color for a flower, you will sometimes find black hollyhocks, irises, narcissus, pansies, and tulips. People who choose black flowers are seeking forgiveness.

Number of Petals

The number of petals on the flower is revealing, too. This relates largely to the person's inner motivation and drive.

One

This is in effect a circle surrounding the flower. People who choose these flowers are honest, loyal, ambitious, and determined. They seek opportunities to progress and are generally better at the overall picture, preferring to leave details to others.

Two

People who choose flowers with two petals are sympathetic, loving, sensitive, diplomatic, and friendly. They seek opportunities to develop their intuition.

Three

People who choose flowers with three petals are friendly, positive, outgoing people who enjoy experiencing all that life has to offer. They seek opportunities to develop their creativity.

Four

People who choose flowers with four petals are responsible, reliable, practical, and determined. They enjoy a regular routine, and are disturbed by change and unexpected upheavals. They seek opportunities to use their down-to-earth practical skills to benefit everyone.

Five

People who choose flowers with five petals enjoy change, variety, travel, and freedom. They have a fear of being hemmed in or restricted. They seek opportunities to use their freedom productively.

Six

People who choose flowers with six petals are responsible, sympathetic, idealistic, and caring. They are devoted to friends and family. They seek opportunities to serve and help others.

Seven

People who choose flowers with seven petals are serious, analytical, idealistic, and spiritual. They seek opportunities to develop mentally and spiritually.

Eight

People who choose flowers with eight petals are ambitious, efficient, reliable, energetic, and confident. They aim high and seek opportunities to achieve their lofty goals.

Nine

People who choose flowers with nine petals are idealistic, romantic, sensitive, and creative. They are natural humanitarians who seek opportunities to help others.

Ten

People who choose flowers with ten petals are ambitious, focused, and independent. They are loners who seek challenges they can pursue with little input from others.

More Than Ten Petals

People who choose flowers with more than ten petals are intelligent, capable, charismatic, and possess a unique approach to problem solving. These people seek opportunities to give and receive universal love.

If the petals of multipetaled flowers can be counted easily, I will count them and reduce the total to a single digit. If the flower has eighteen petals, for instance, I add the 1 and 8, and interpret the flower as if it had nine petals. However, if the flower has too many petals to count quickly or easily, I use the interpretation for flowers with more than ten petals.

Scent

The strength of the flower's perfume provides additional insights. A delicate fragrance is gentler than a stronger, brasher perfume. People who choose flowers with a strong scent are impatient and desire quick results. Similarly, people who choose flowers with a more delicate scent are more patient and willing to allow whatever time is necessary to achieve their aims. Some flowers have no discernible scent. In this case, aroma—or lack of it—is ignored.

I find it interesting that some people select their flowers largely by the scent, while others choose by look and appearance.

Stalk

Sometimes people will show you a flower without any stalk. This is rare, though. Usually, at least part of the stalk is still attached, and this can be interpreted. The bottom third of the stalk relates to the past, and valuable information can be obtained by looking at how the stalk was removed from the plant. If it has been cut off, the person's childhood was smooth and happy. However, the person's childhood was difficult if the stalk was roughly cut or torn from the plant. The middle third relates to the present. Look for any knots or imperfections on the stalk in this section. These indicate current problems. The top third, closest to the flower, indicates the future.

Putting It Together

Let's assume a twenty-five-year-old man named Tom has come to you for a flower reading. You probably expect him to hand you a beautiful rose or perhaps an orchid. Instead, he hands you a daisy. I am using this as the first example because daisies will be handed to you surprisingly often.

I start by looking at the condition of the flower. Has it been picked carefully? Is the flower damaged in any way? Is the flower aesthetically pleasing?

I then take note of the five areas: theme, shape, color, number of petals, and scent.

Theme: innocence. Tom is likely to be innocent, possibly naïve. He requires patience and strength to handle a difficult situation.

Shape: sun. Flowers of this shape are related to confidence and self-expression. This means Tom has to accept his personal power, become less serious, and be willing to express himself openly.

Color: white. White relates to purity, innocence, and forgiveness. Tom is releasing negativity and filling his mind with feelings of freedom, hope, and endless opportunities. He is likely to be undergoing some sort of transformation in his life.

The center of the flower is yellow. This shows Tom wants to communicate and interact well with others.

Number of petals: more than ten. Tom's choice shows he is intelligent, capable, charismatic, and possesses a unique approach to problem solving. He is looking for opportunities to give and receive universal love.

Scent: delicate. Tom is patient and prepared to allow whatever time is necessary for changes to occur.

Tom has chosen his daisy well. He has left a long stalk, the daisy itself is well-formed, and each petal is perfect. This reveals care and attention to detail.

You might say to him: "It looks to me as if you're about to start something new. You're feeling somewhat nervous about it, but fortunately you have the necessary confidence and strength to carry it through. You'll be able to bring your rather unusual approach to problem solving to this task. However, you'll probably also have to 'lighten up' a bit, as it looks as if you can be overly serious at times. You have been holding on to something from the past, but you are in a transformation stage and you're letting it go. Forgiveness of yourself and others will do you a world of good. Your communication skills will stand you in good stead during this transitional period. It's fortunate that you're patient, as you'll need patience from time to time. Despite occasional setbacks, you're going to make huge progress in the next few months."

Here's another example. Sophia is a fifty-eight-year-old woman. She hands you a pink camellia. The petals are fluffy and arranged in concentric circles, telling you it is a fountain-shaped flower. She has chosen a perfectly formed flower.

Theme: There is no specific theme attached to the camellia, but it is generally associated with love. A white camellia symbolizes a chaste love, and a red flower indicates passion ("you are a flame in my heart"). A pink camellia indicates admiration and longing. Sophia may well be fond of someone, but she has probably not yet revealed her feelings to the other person.

Shape: fountain. This shows Sophia is friendly, open-minded, loving, and curious. However, she is also likely to be cautious and shy. This makes it even more likely that she has not yet expressed her feelings.

Color: pink. Pink is an innocent yet positive, cheerful, nurturing, and loving color. It is a calming and soothing color that encourages positive thoughts about the future. People who choose pink flowers desire more love in their lives. Sophia is probably lonely and craves friendship.

Number of petals: As there are far too many petals to count, you use the "more than ten" guideline. This shows that Sophia is intelligent and has a unique approach to problem solving. She seeks opportunities to give and receive universal love.

Scent: Camellias have no discernible perfume. Violetta, the heroine of Verdi's opera *La Traviata*, wore camellias because she had been forced to sell her jewelry. Violetta was based on Madeleine de Plessis, a nineteenth century Parisian courtesan who wore camellias since scented flowers made her cough. This may have been an early indication of the consumption that ultimately killed her.

What should you say to Sophia? Here's one possibility: "You are intelligent and use your unique way of thinking extremely well. However, it looks as if you've been holding yourself back for far too long. I know you've experienced sorrow in the past and have probably been hurt by others. There are obviously good reasons for your caution. Choosing a pink camellia tells me that inwardly you want to move forward in your life again. It's time for you to become a little more assertive and tell someone what you really feel. This will make two people very happy. There's no need to do this today, but don't wait too long. Your sense of caution is usually a good friend, but sometimes it can prevent you from doing something that might bring great happiness. You do have a great deal of happiness in your future, but you have to make the first small step first."

Day of the Week

Many people choose their flower on a certain day of the week. This adds the purpose of the day to the interpretation of the flower. In practice, I seldom use this but I am including it for completeness. I use this only when I know the person is concerned with an important matter and needs as much help as possible.

Certain flowers and perfumes have also been associated with the days of the week, and some people like to use these associations. Obviously, this is not always possible. I think it is better to choose a flower that feels right for you rather than choosing one that has traditionally been associated with the day.

Sunday

Planet: sun

Plant: sunflower

Perfume: myrrh, saffron

You should choose a flower on Sunday if your question relates to creativity, divination, authority, or financial matters.

Monday

Planet: moon

Plant: peony

Perfume: camphor, white sandalwood

You should choose your flower on Monday if your question relates to news from afar, reconciliation, or dealings with women.

Tuesday

Planet: Mars

Plant: rue

Perfume: benzoin, sulphur

You should choose your flower on Tuesday if your question involves courage, energy, action, or any dealings with potential enemies.

Wednesday

Planet: Mercury

Plant: cinquefoil

Perfume: narcissus

You should choose your flower on Wednesday if your question relates to communication, criticism, the intellect, science, or buying or selling.

Thursday

Planet: Jupiter

Plant: agrimony

Perfume: balm, nutmeg

You should choose your flower on Thursday if your question relates to expansion of any sort, abundance, or good fortune. Thursday is also good for handling religious or philosophical matters.

Friday

Planet: Venus

Plant: vervain

Perfume: ambergris, pink rose

You should choose your flower on Friday if your question relates to friendship, love, marriage, or pleasant pastimes.

Saturday

Planet: Saturn

Plant: houseleek

Perfume: musk, alum

You should choose your flower on Saturday if your question relates to learning, possessions, money owing and owed, or persistence and agriculture.

Other Forms of Flower Divination

For hundreds of years, children have used flowers to play "he/she loves me, he/she loves me not." Kids usually blow on a dandelion seed pod, but sometimes they pull the petals off a daisy. Both of these methods can be used by adults seeking an answer to an important question. Dandelions are particularly useful for timing an event. Decide if you are asking for days, weeks, or months before starting to blow. The number of blows it takes to release all of the seeds will provide your answer.

Twin roses

This method is useful if you need to make a choice between two options. Purchase two identical rosebuds and place them in long-stemmed glasses. It is important that the rosebuds are completely closed. Place them side by side in a warm position that is not overly sunny. Write down the two possibilities you have to choose from on two pieces of paper, and place one under each vase. The first rose to bloom fully will indicate the choice you should make.

The first time I tried this, both roses bloomed at exactly the same time. If this occurs, watch to see which flower fades more slowly. This indicates the correct choice.

• • •

Many people are surprised that you can read trees as well as flowers. We'll look at tree reading in the next chapter.

ten

Tree Reading

*T*rees are one of the most frequently found symbols in the world. This is not surprising, since an ancient oak tree, for instance, symbolizes strength as well as wisdom and knowledge. An aspen appears to be trembling with fear. A palm tree symbolizes warmth and adventure. A fruit tree symbolizes fecundity and fruitfulness. A tree can even symbolize a person rooted in their earthly life but reaching for the sky and, hopefully, spiritual awareness.

The Druids performed a tree divination called *dendromancy* that used oak and mistletoe. Mistletoe and branches of oak were collected and burned. It was a good sign if they burned quickly and if the smoke rose up quickly into the sky. The indications were not so good if the smoke failed to rise.

We are not going to read or burn real trees in this chapter. The form of tree reading we're going to discuss in this chapter is something I've been fascinated with for many years. I find it surprising that so few people know anything about it.

For almost twenty years I read palms at the Easter show (something like a county fair) in the city where I live. Many people came every year for a reading, and some of them ultimately became friends. One of these was a middle-aged lady who demonstrated and sold vacuum cleaners at the show. She always came for a reading on the first day of every show.

After reading her palms for several years, she told me that she read trees and if I'd draw her a tree, she'd interpret it for me. When I had some free time I drew a tree and gave it to her. As we were both busy, she wrote down her interpretation and gave it to me on the following day. As I'd studied graphology, I was aware of the amount of information we reveal about ourselves whenever we write something or sign our name. However, I'd always associated this with words rather than with pictures. I was amazed at how much insight she was able to deduce about my character from my simple drawing of a tree.

I have always been fascinated with different systems of divination and character analysis, and so I arranged to have some lessons from her once the show was over. At one stage, this lady was going to write a small book on the subject of tree reading but decided against it because her religious husband was opposed to the idea.

Psychologists have used picture-drawing techniques for at least eighty years. In 1926, Florence Goodenough (1886–1959) published her findings on determining the intelligence of children by analyzing their drawings of a man.[22] Shortly after this, Emil Jucker began using tree drawings to help people find the right vocation. Karl Koch, a Swiss psychiatrist, greatly expanded on this concept by using tree drawing to help school students decide on the correct type of career for them.[23] In 1948, John Buck, a clinical psychologist, published his House-Tree-Person (H–T–P) Projective Technique, which involved drawing a house, a tree, and a person.[24] In Japan, Kimio Yoshikawa and several colleagues also studied tree reading.[25] Since 1987, Dr. K. Loganathan of Universiti Sains Malaysia has been advancing the work of Kimio Yoshikawa with his "New Baum Test." This involves drawing four trees, all bearing fruit. The first is a simple tree drawing. The second is a tree drawn as realistically as possible. The third is an imaginary tree. The final drawing is a fantasy tree that is entirely different from any tree found in the real world.[26]

22. Florence Laura Goodenough, *Measurement of Intelligence by Drawing* (New York: World Book Company, 1926).

23. Karl Koch, *Der Baumtest: Der Baumzeichenversuch als Psychodiagnostisches Hilfsmittel* [The Tree Test: The Tree-Drawing Test as an Aid in Psychodiagnosis] (Berne, Switzerland: Verlag H. Huber, 1957). (Originally published in 1935.)

24. John N. Buck, *The House-Tree-Person Technique* (Los Angeles: Western Psychological Services, 1948).

25. Y. Huzioka and Kimio Yoshikawa. "Image Expression by Tree Test," *Anthropological Standpoint Quarterly Anthropologist* (Tokyo, 1971), 2 (3): 3–28.

26. Dr. K. Loganathan, *Agamic Psychology: The Baum Test and Hermeneutic Semiotics.* Available online at http://www.tamil.net/list/2000-06/msg00061.html (accessed 18 March 2008).

Tree reading is not only revealing but also great fun to do. Before reading any further, pause and draw a tree. You will be able to analyze it as you go through the twelve-step process.

Size of the Tree

The first step is to see how large the tree is compared to the size of the sheet of paper it is drawn on. A small tree indicates someone who is cautious, careful, and thrifty. These people never buy anything without looking around for the cheapest price.

People who draw large trees are generous and willing to give of themselves. Overly generous people draw trees so large that they don't fit onto the paper. These people find it hard to say no.

Placement

A tree that is placed in the middle of the page indicates someone who is well-organized and thinks before acting.

If the tree is placed on the top half of the page, the person is inclined to be a dreamer. This person has a restless nature and needs more space and room around them than most people.

If the tree is placed in the bottom half of the page, the person is down-to-earth, capable, reliable, and practical.

If the tree is placed on the left-hand side of the page, the artist is introverted. The person is an extrovert if the tree is placed on the right-hand side of the page.

Occasionally, someone will turn the sheet of paper ninety degrees before drawing the tree. This person is independent and broad-minded.

Detail

Some people draw trees using just a few lines. Others include a great deal of detail. A simple sketch of a tree using few lines indicates someone who prefers the broad overview of things and prefers leaving the details to others. Someone who draws a tree with a great deal of detail enjoys detailed work and will be something of a perfectionist and enjoy doing everything properly.

A few people will draw a tree that is so simple that it hardly resembles a tree. These people are trying to conceal their inner selves.

Shading

Shading indicates the drawer is introspective and serious. Sometimes you will be shown a tree that is shaded or darkened in just one part. This shows the person has concerns or issues about a certain area of their life. A shaded trunk reveals concerns about the person's home and family life. Shaded roots indicate problems and difficulties in the past. Shading at the top of the tree indicates worries about the future.

Pressure

Some people use a great deal of force when drawing, while others use very little. Drawings by people who use a great deal of pressure can be felt from the other side of the paper. Pressure reveals the mental energy the person is putting in to the drawing.

Heavy pressure indicates someone who is intense, forceful, aggressive, energetic, assertive, and determined. This person also possesses plenty of vitality and likes to be in charge or in control of any situation.

Light pressure indicates someone who is gentle, sensitive, unassertive, passive, and self-effacing. This person will tend to avoid confrontation and will work best in a harmonious environment.

Most people fall between these two extremes, which means they are moderately confident and like people. They are friendly, open, and easy to get along with.

A few people use both firm and light pressure on the same drawing. This indicates nervousness. The drawer might be worried about what you might read in the drawing.

Shape

Shapes of trees vary enormously. A tall tree, such as a fir, indicates someone who is positive, ambitious, and is aiming high. A point at the top of the tree affirms and strengthens this.

A short, wide tree reveals that the person is stable, content, and satisfied with life.

A naturally protective person will draw a tree that is extremely wide compared to its height. Mothering, caring people will draw a tree of this sort.

A tree that appears to be swaying or bending in the breeze indicates someone who is full of energy. This person enjoys being involved in many different activities.

Base

Many people draw trees that appear to be floating in midair. This indicates a spontaneous person who easily goes with the flow of life.

Someone who anchors their tree in the ground has a need for stability and security. Such a person likes to prepare ahead to eliminate any potential surprises.

If the ground is indicated as a slightly curving line attached to, or close to, the base of the tree, the person will be contented and happy.

A noticeably slanting base indicates insecurity.

Those who have deliberately or subconsciously cut themselves off from the past will draw a straight line at the base of the tree.

A tree planted on the top of a hill indicates a desire for attention. This person wants to be seen and admired.

A tree planted in a pot indicates someone who is ready to move at a moment's notice. Such a person will be spontaneous, fun-loving, and sometimes exhausting.

Roots

Roots indicate a strong association with the past. Past influences are still playing an important part in this person's life. Pleasant-looking roots indicate happy memories from childhood. The influences from this person's past are still stable, strong, and supportive. Dark, ugly, or gnarled roots indicate unhappy childhood memories.

An absence of roots reveals that the past is not of great importance in the person's life. Their strength comes from what they are today.

Trunk

The trunk denotes the person's personal strength and conscious mind. A wide, strong-looking trunk denotes someone who is independent and can stand up to anything life has to offer, good or bad.

A slim trunk reveals someone who is flexible and adaptable. This person will be gentle, loving, and kind. This person will bend, cooperate or even give in if necessary.

A straight trunk denotes someone who is well-organized and efficient in all areas of life.

If the trunk is clear and relatively unmarked, the person enjoys a happy home and family life. If it is gnarled, twisted, and shaded, then the person is unhappy with their home and family life.

A knothole in the trunk denotes someone who forgives others readily. This person accepts others as they are. However, if the knothole is dark and well-shaded, the person is hard on herself or himself.

If the trunk has a split in the base, the person is still haunted by unpleasant memories from the past.

Treetop

A round treetop, like an apple, indicates people who are private and like to keep part of themselves hidden.

A fluffy treetop, similar to a cloud, denotes a friendly, happy person who enjoys life.

A tree containing branches but no foliage reveals an honest person who likes to ensure that everything has a good foundation.

However, a bare tree with drooping branches indicates sadness and possibly depression.

A tree that contains both branches and leaves indicates someone who is concerned with the whole picture.

If the treetop is made up of many individually drawn leaves, the person likes to have everything in life organized well.

If the branches point skyward, the person looks forward rather than backward. This person is always interested in what the future has to offer.

If the branches spread out in a variety of directions, the person is sociable and enjoys interacting with others.

Additions

Many people enjoy adding other features, either to the tree or to the nearby area.

Grass growing under the tree is very common and indicates that the person wants their home to be friendly, inviting, and comfortable.

Flowers growing under the tree indicate the person enjoys beautiful things and will fill their home with attractive items. It is usually an indication of happiness.

Birds, animals, and people show the person is friendly and enjoys company.

Fruits and nuts on the tree show the person enjoys their home and family life. This person also needs to feel that what they do is productive and worthwhile.

A sun shining above the tree indicates a positive, optimistic person.

Clouds show the person expects a number of disappointments and unhappy experiences as they progress through life.

A swing hanging from the tree reveals a strong sense of fun and play. This person seeks fun and pleasure in every aspect of life.

A large number of individually drawn leaves indicate stress and worry.

A leaf, fruit, or branch falling from the tree indicates sadness.

Special Trees

Someone who draws a Christmas tree will be nostalgic, sentimental, and traditional. This person will look forward to celebrations of all kinds.

A palm tree reveals an ambitious dreamer. This person will dream big dreams and then pursue them.

People who feel sad, lonely, or are hanging on to something from the past frequently draw willow trees.

Johann's Reading

Johann is a twenty-six-year-old self-employed builder. His parents were killed in a car accident when he was four years old, and he was brought up by an elderly great-aunt who looked after his physical needs but neglected everything else. Johann was teased at school and left as soon as he could. After a few years of menial work, he decided to make something of his life and became a builder. He loves his work and because he is good at it, he has done well. Johann has never had a serious relationship and is extremely shy with women. He is friendly once you get to know him, but he is basically shy and introverted. I met Johann because he is a friend of one of my sons. I was curious as to what sort of tree he would draw.

It was an informal social gathering, and the topic of tree reading had somehow come up in the conversation. Almost everyone drew a tree, as they were keen to find out about themselves. Johann hesitated before agreeing to draw a tree. Unlike the others, he went into another room and drew his tree there.

At first glance his tree looked fine. It was centered on the sheet of paper and had a large, broad trunk. The branches looked like fluffy clouds. However, he had shaded them with strong angry strokes. A single strong line drawn at a sharp angle attached the base of the tree to the ground. He had used a mixture of light and heavy pressure while drawing his tree.

The wide, broad trunk showed Johann could stand up to anything life could throw at him. This was not surprising, as he'd learned to stand on his own two feet at a very young age. I was momentarily surprised at the fluffy, cloud-like appearance of the branches, as these tend to denote an outgoing, friendly person. However, the heavy shading inside the cloud-like shape showed he was basically introspective and serious. The shading was extremely strong and showed he was a worrier. The pressure he used and the jagged patterns he created with the shading indicated a well-hidden inner anger and stress. The line that attached his tree to the ground was at a forty-five degree angle. This revealed Johann's insecurity.

Anna's Tree

Anna is an attractive forty-five-year-old woman. She exercises every day and looks years younger than her actual age. She is divorced with two teenage children, and is living with a new partner.

When I asked her to draw a tree, she drew a single line for the trunk and added a circle at the top to represent the branches. Her drawing looked more like a lollipop than a tree. Her tree was drawn in the top third of the sheet of paper, and it was created with minimal pressure.

The lack of pressure and the placement of the tree indicated a gentle, sensitive person who spent much of her time in a world of dreams. The tree was small, indicating someone who was cautious and thought carefully before acting. The lack of detail showed she prefers a broad overview of a situation rather than all the details. In this example, Anna's drawing indicated that she was trying to conceal, rather than reveal, anything about herself. The lack of a base to her tree shows that Anna has a spontaneous approach to life. The lack of roots shows that Anna lives in the present and is not overly concerned with the past. A single line for the trunk shows Anna is flexible and cooperative. She can adapt or bend if necessary. A round circle to represent the treetop shows Anna is secretive and likes to keep part of herself hidden.

Anna agreed with this assessment. "I'm reasonably outgoing," she told me. "I like to have a good time. But there's part of me that always holds back, whether I want to or not. I'm not spontaneous. I need a reason to do things. I've had bad times in the past, but they're in the past. I hardly ever think about them. I'm happy living in the here and now. I'd probably be happier if I could open up a bit more, but that's not me. I think I understand myself well, and over the years I've come to accept myself as I am."

Change Your Tree, Change Your Life

If you are not happy with what your tree reveals about you, you have the power to change it. It is not easy to do, but it can be done. Choose the qualities you want to possess and deliberately draw a tree that represents them. Once you are happy with your new tree, draw the same tree every day for at least twenty-eight days. As you do this, you will find yourself gradually changing in small ways. Ultimately, you will start projecting the qualities you wish to possess, and they will become a normal, natural part of your life.

Someone once told me he thought this was cheating, as I was asking him to deliberately draw trees that did not reflect him. He called the idea "phony." I disagreed; the trees reflected the future the person desired. We all have the ability to improve our lives in many different ways, and this is one way in which we can effect good, positive change.

Drawing and interpreting trees can make you hungry. In the next chapter we'll discuss how to use plants to create foods for love.

eleven

Foods for Love

hroughout history people have searched for effective aphrodisiacs and potions to captivate and entrance prospective
lovers. Medieval herbals contain many recipes relating to love and
romance. "Herball tonickes" were also created to cure impotence,
frigidity, sterility, and other problems relating to sex.

As well as potions, many foods were considered "foods of love."
Ever since Paris presented Venus with a golden apple, the fruit has
been associated with love. Although the "fruit of the tree" that Eve
offered Adam was not specifically named, John Milton wrote that it
was an apple in his epic poem *Paradise Lost*:

> Till, on a day roving the field, I chanced
> A goodly tree far distant to behold
> Loaden with fruit of fairest colours mixed,
> Ruddy and gold: I nearer drew to gaze;
> When from the boughs a savoury odour blown,
> Grateful to appetite, more pleased my sense
> Than smell of sweetest fennel, or the teats
> Of ewe or goat dropping with milk at even,
> Unsucked of lamb or kid, that tend their play.
> To satisfy the sharp desire I had
> Of tasting those fair apples, I resolved
> Not to defer; hunger and thirst at once,
> Powerful persuaders, quickened at the scent
> Of that alluring fruit, urged me so keen.
> About the mossy trunk I wound me soon;
> For, high from ground, the branches would require
> Thy utmost reach or Adam's: round the tree
> All other beasts that saw, with like desire
> Longing and envying stood, but could not reach.

> Amid the tree now got, where plenty hung
> Tempting so nigh, to pluck and eat my fill
> I spared not; for, such pleasure till that hour,
> At feed or fountain, never had I found.

Dr. Sigmund Freud associated the apple, and all round fruits, with the breast. Consequently, as it might date back to Adam and Eve, the apple could have been the first symbol of love. Horace (65–8 BCE), the poet and satirist, wrote about a form of love magic using apple pips. Lovers used their thumbs and first fingers to propel an apple pip up to the ceiling. If the pip hit the ceiling, their love was reciprocated.[27]

When the tomato was introduced to Europe from Mexico in the sixteenth century, it was called a "love apple" because of its reputed aphrodisiacal qualities. When Oliver Cromwell came to power, the Puritans discouraged the eating of "love apples" as they encouraged immorality. To ensure people stopped eating them, they also spread a rumor that tomatoes were poisonous. This worked so well that few people were prepared to eat tomatoes until the middle of the nineteenth century.

The truffle, a fungus that grows on the roots of trees, has been considered an aphrodisiac since Roman times. The French writer Anthelme Brillat-Savarin wrote that truffles awaken "erotic and gastronomic ideas both in the sex wearing petticoats and in the bearded portion of humanity."[28]

The Greeks were great believers in the aphrodisiacal qualities of the onion. Strangely, they never considered mushrooms to be aphrodisiacs, possibly because they were sacred plants.

The Romans used beans as aphrodisiacs, and because of this the supposedly ascetic followers of Pythagoras were not allowed to eat them.

The Chinese have used ginseng as an aphrodisiac for thousands of years. Nowadays ginseng is widely advertised on the Internet, showing that it is still sought after.

---

27.   Horace, *The Satires of Horace and Persius* (London: Penguin, 1973), 2:3.

28.   Anthelme Brillat-Savarin, *The Physiology of Taste* (London: Constable and Company, 1960). Originally published in French as *La Physiologie du Goût*, 1825.

In Elizabethan England, carrots, potatoes, dates, and quinces were all used as aphrodisiacs. In his *Herball*, published in 1597, John Gerard wrote of the carrot "serving in love matters." Elizabethan brothels gave clients prunes free of charge to help them achieve their goals.[29]

How to Attract a Partner

Valerian has a pleasing scent that has been used for hundreds of years to attract a love interest. A single woman would quickly attract suitors if she carried a sprig of valerian with her. Interestingly, valerian also works for other members of the animal kingdom. The Pied Piper of Hamelin used valerian to lure the rats away from the town.

Young women knew that if they applied a paste of foxgloves and belladonna to the eyelids of a sleeping man, he would propose marriage as soon as he woke up.

An old love divination says that twelve leaves of sage should be picked at midnight on Midsummer's Eve. The person's future partner should appear as the twelfth leaf is picked.

If you place a sprig of rosemary and a coin under your pillow, you will see your future partner in your dreams.

An alternative to this is to walk backward around a pear tree nine times. After doing this, you should see an image of your future partner.

The Romans believed that sprinkling rose petals over a man's grave would enable women to see their future lover.

An interesting possibility is to prick an orange all over with a needle, place it in your left armpit, and then enjoy a good night's sleep. In the morning, present the orange to the person you adore. If they eat it, you can rest assured your lover will remain true to you.

---

29. Edward S. Gifford, *The Charms of Love* (London: Faber and Faber, 1962), 186.

How to Ensure Your Partner Is Truthful

If a young man is wearing a buttonhole containing belladonna that was given to him by his lover, he will be unable to tell a lie.

How to Ensure Your Partner Remains Faithful

Polish brides used to dig up earth from their husbands' footprints and place it in a window box. They then sowed marigold seeds in it. The woman's husband would stay faithful to her as long as the flowers bloomed. Naturally, she had to continue sowing seeds every now and again to ensure a continuity of flowers.

A Welsh tradition involves a twig of lemon balm. This was split in two and each partner carried one piece in a small cloth bag as a lucky charm that ensured faithfulness.

A similar tradition suggests that newlyweds break a branch of laurel. As long as each partner retains their piece, the marriage will last.

Italian girls used cumin seed to keep their partners faithful. If her lover was about to go away for any length of time, she would bake him a loaf of bread seasoned with cumin seeds. To make absolutely certain, she might also give him a bottle of wine that had powdered cumin added to it.

According to tradition, the Virgin Mary draped her cloak over a rosemary bush during the flight to Egypt. The formerly white flowers immediately changed to match the blue of her cloak. Consequently, if a bride gives her husband a sprig of rosemary on their honeymoon, he will remain faithful and impervious to temptation.

How to Revive Lost Passion

If the sexual element has waned in a relationship, a medieval German remedy might work. The wife has to make bread on nine different occasions, and save a small amount of raw dough each time. After this, she must make a scone with the nine pieces of dough and give it to her husband to eat. This will, apparently, create a second honeymoon for the couple.

Encouraging an Errant Lover to Return

If your lover has left you for another, you can encourage them to return by picking three red roses on Midsummer's Eve. You need to bury one under a yew tree, the second in a newly dug grave, and the third rose must be placed under your pillow. After three nights, your lover will see you every night in their dreams. The dreams will become more and more intense until your lover finally returns home again.

Love Charms

Attracting the right partner is one thing; keeping them is another. Young women in Europe wore fenugreek around their necks when they were with their boyfriends. This kept him faithful and stopped him from looking at other women.

Pennyroyal used to be sprinkled on beds to act as a love charm. Bananas and carrots have also been used as love charms because of their phallic shapes.

The ancient Romans believed that the scent of burning vervain and frankincense would arouse even the coldest woman.

Aphrodisiacs

Garlic has always been considered a powerful aphrodisiac, as it cleanses the blood and provides plenty of stamina.

The Chinese have always used ginseng as an aphrodisiac. It was also used as a remedy to cure impotency.

Shakespeare appeared to promote the aphrodisiacal qualities of caraway in *Henry IV, Part 2* (act 5, scene 3) when he had Shallow say, "[I]n an arbour, we will eat a last year's pippin [apple] of my own graffing, with a dish of caraways, and so forth: come, cousin Silence: and then to bed."

In *The Arabian Nights*, coriander is mentioned as an aphrodisiac. The seeds were popularly used for this purpose during the Renaissance.

The Greeks considered the pomegranate a symbol of fertility and love. They fed pomegranate seeds to young women, believing this would encourage licentiousness and debauchery.

A number of vegetables have been considered aphrodisiacs, too. These include lettuce, onions, potatoes, radishes, and tomatoes.

Regaining Virginity

Women who regretted the loss of their virginity could restore it by sitting in a bath containing a liquid made by boiling comfrey.

Ensuring Pregnancy

Wine made from sage was believed to increase women's fertility. After any major loss of life, such as a war, Hippocrates (c. 460– c. 377 BCE), known as the father of medicine, recommended all women drink it to increase the population again.

A woman who is given a parsley plant is believed to become pregnant within twelve months.

Ginger was considered an important remedy for women who couldn't conceive. In China, hot ginger wine is served to women who have given birth to their first child.

• • •

It is now time to look at the world of fairies. Many people believe fairies look after, and are responsible for, the beauty and life of the plant kingdom.

twelve

Flower Fairies

hroughout history many people have believed in a race of immortal beings known as fairies. They are usually considered to be tiny beings in the shape of people. Some fairies are strikingly beautiful, while others, such as dwarfs and goblins, are usually hideous. There are many accounts of fairies in medieval European folklore. Dwarfs known as *ground-manikins* live in Germany but are seldom seen. Beautiful fairies known as *wild women* live in Austria. They love children, and have been known to steal human children when their parents are distracted. In Switzerland, friendly fairies known as *hill men* actively help people and sometimes provide gifts of cheese. This cheese is extremely useful—whenever a piece is eaten, it instantly restores itself to a whole cheese again. In the summer, hill-men enjoy watching humans at work.[30]

In Persia, two races of fairies, known as *deeves* and *peris*, endlessly fought each other. The peris were friendly to humans, and the female peris were believed to be so beautiful that not even poets could adequately describe them. The genii, or *djinns*, of Arabia are well known. Humans can confine them inside objects such as lamps, and summon them to do their bidding by rubbing on the imprisoning container. Trolls are trouble-making dwarfs in Scandinavia. Good and bad elves can be found in Norway.

People have always believed that flowers and plants possess spirits that can appear to humans in various guises. Each spirit has its own personality and role to perform. This concept of a parallel universe is confusing to some, but people who have seen and worked with fairies and nature spirits see nothing strange in the belief that all living things possess a spiritual consciousness.

Flower fairies are possibly the most beautiful of all nature spirits. Their task is to look after their plant and to encourage humans to live in harmony with all life. Some flower fairies look after an entire plant, while others are responsible for a single flower.

---

30. Julian Franklyn (editor), *A Dictionary of the Occult* (New York: Causeway Books, 1973), 99.

Flower fairies have played a major role in the folklore and literature of many countries. In sixteenth and seventeenth century England, flower fairies attended to the needs of the Fairy King and Queen. By the end of the nineteenth century, the emphasis had shifted, and flower fairies were believed to provide the beautiful coloring of the flowers and provide pleasing scents in the nighttime air. They also protected young lovers and ensured the fertility of all nature. However, the fairies would cause the crops to be blighted if they felt ignored or insulted by humans.

The word *fairy* comes from the Latin word *Fata*, which means "the Fates." The word *fey*, to mean someone who is clairvoyant, also comes from the same Latin root. Interestingly, I discovered while living in Scotland that many people there use the word *fey* to describe someone who is fated to die.

Flower fairies are believed to wear the same colors as their guardian flower. In fact, it is the other way around. Flowers display the same colors as their personal fairy.

Primroses have always been prized, partly because they are the first flowers of spring. In Ireland, people plant primroses outside their front doors to attract good luck and to ward off evil forces. A bouquet of primroses must contain at least thirteen flowers, as a smaller bouquet creates bad luck. An old English folktale tells of a young girl who became lost in a forest while out picking primroses. As soon as she added the thirteenth primrose to her bouquet, hundreds of yellow fairies appeared in order to escort her back home. They also gave her several beautiful gifts. One of her neighbors became jealous after hearing her story and decided to visit the fairies himself. Unfortunately, he picked less than thirteen primroses, and he never returned home.

Another legend says that if you pick hyacinths in the woods on your own, you will be captured and held prisoner by the fairies until someone you love comes looking for you.

Because fairies make their homes in trees, it is important to treat all trees with respect. Arguably, their favorite tree is the hawthorn, but they also like alder, ash, beech, elder, oak, and rowan trees. In the classical world, tree fairies or wood nymphs were known as *hamadryads*. The word *hamadryad* was often shortened to *dryad*. Dryads are playful fairies who enjoy helping—and sometimes teasing—human beings. They are most active at the time of the full moon. Dryads looked after their tree, and died if the tree was chopped down.

The best time to contact flower fairies is at the time of the spring equinox. This is when they wake up after their long winter hibernation and help in the annual rebirth of nature.

Devas

Deva is a Sanskrit word that means "shining one." Devas are the life force within nature. There is an oak tree deva, for instance. There is also a carrot deva, a pineapple deva, and so on. Flower fairies, or nature spirits, are more regional than devas. The devic energies of an apple tree in China, New Zealand, or the United States are identical, as they all connect with the apple deva. In other words, devic energies are international. Nature spirits work alongside devas to ensure that your specific part of the world is looked after.

George Washington Carver (1864–1943), the American botanist, worked extensively with nature spirits and learned from them everything he needed to know to make constructive and practical use of the peanut.

The famous gardens at Findhorn, Scotland were developed in the 1970s, and are a perfect example of people working with devic energies. The Perelandra Gardens, established by Machaelle Small Wright, also in the 1970s, are less well-known but equally as successful. Perelandra is situated sixty miles southwest of Washington, DC, in the foothills of the Blue Ridge Mountains in Virginia. It covers forty-five acres of fields, woods, streams, and gardens. When Machaelle established her garden, she meditated each day to establish a connection with the devic level. A deva would enter her awareness, introduce itself, and tell her what seeds to buy, which fertilizer to use, where to plant the seeds and how far apart they should be, when to thin the plants, and everything else she needed to know. Over a period of time she found she could identify the vibration of individual devas, and she could call on the specific devas she wanted to talk with.

In the process of working with her garden, Machaelle discovered an entirely new way of working with healing energies. She calls this "co-creative science," the science of working in full, conscious cooperation with nature intelligences. Perelandra is open to the public just once a year, as its primary purpose is nature research.

Elementals

The elementals are the spirits of the four elements of fire, earth, air, and water. Some people call *all* nature spirits elementals. However, the term should really only be used when referring to the spirits of the four elements. Paracelsus (1493–1541), the famous Swiss alchemist and physician, named the elementals as salamanders (fire), gnomes (earth), sylphs (air), and undines (water). These elementals live in a parallel universe between the spiritual and material worlds, and provide magical energies that can be channeled and used by human beings.

Salamanders, the elemental spirits of fire, live in fires and areas of volcanic activity. They are dragon-like beings that live in flames. People often see them as sparks or flashes of color. The word *salamander* comes from the Greek word *salambe*, which means "fireplace." The fire element relates to ambition, career, energy, goals, passion, and sex. Salamanders are able to change shape as quickly as fire. Salamanders can be called upon to help with courage, creativity, inspiration, and purification. A good way to call on salamanders for help is to meditate in front of a lit candle.

Gnomes, the elemental spirits of earth, frequently appear in fairy stories as dwarves who live underground. The earth element relates to food, health, nourishment, and wealth. Gnomes look after the treasures of the earth, such as crystals and gemstones. The word *gnome* is derived from the Greek word *genomus*, which means "earth-dweller." As the king of the gnomes is named Gob, gnomes are sometimes referred to as goblins. Gnomes can be called upon to help with earth magic, fertility, herbal healing, prosperity, and protection. The easiest way to contact them is to spend time outdoors in the earth element. You may find it helpful to hold a crystal or stone when asking the earth elementals for help.

Sylphs, the elementals of air, are winged beings who live on top of mountains. They can often be found in winds, clouds, rain, storms, and snowflakes. The word *sylph* comes from the Greek word *silphe*, which means "butterfly." The air element relates to communication, education, music, thought, and wisdom. Sylphs can be called upon by burning incense or fragrant oils. They also respond well to music. Sylphs provide assistance with communication, learning, and travel.

Undines, the elementals of water, live in water. They are often found in waterfalls, springs, and streams but can also be found in rivers, lakes, oceans, and anywhere else there is a body of water. Undines are graceful beings and look similar to mermaids. The word *undine* comes from the Latin word *unda*, which means "wave." The water element relates to dreams, emotions, intuition, and imagination. Undines can be called upon by scrying. Today, scrying is normally associated with a crystal ball, but originally scrying was performed by gazing into a pool of clear water. Undines can be called upon to help with matters relating to children, family life, love, psychic development, relationships, and sex. The easiest way to contact undines is to spend time beside an attractive body of water. You may want to make a small offering of a posy of flowers. Undines will contact you through your emotions.

Shamans from all cultures are able to experience elementals by entering an altered state, usually by drumming or dancing. Most people in the West find it easier to contact elementals by relaxing and meditating until they can see them in their mind's eye.

How to Contact Fairies

Fairies can be unpredictable, and you need to approach them with caution. When I lived in Cornwall, England in the 1960s, I was warned that visitors to remote wooded areas could be captured by fairies, elves, and pixies. People became hopelessly lost, even in small groves of trees, and found it impossible to escape. This was the locals' advice about what to do in this situation: turn your coat or jacket inside out and place your right shoe on your left foot. Hopping on this foot thirteen times broke the spell.

Ernest Thompson Seton (1860–1946) wrote a beautiful poem called "The Road to Fairyland," which explained how to get to Fairyland:

> Did you see the road to Fairyland
> I'll tell, it's easy, quite
> Wait till a yellow moon gets up
> O'er purple seas by night,
> And gilds a shining pathway
> That is sparkling diamond bright
> Then, if no evil power be nigh
> To thwart you, out of spite,
> And if you know the very words
> To cast a spell of might,
> You get upon a thistledown,
> And if the breeze is right,
> You sail away to Fairyland
> Along this track of light.[31]

The best times to find fairies are at dawn and dusk. According to folklore, you can create a mixture of ingredients to dab onto your eyes to help you see fairies more clearly. Half fill a small container with rainwater. Place a rose, a marigold, and your favorite flower

---

31. Ernest Thompson Seton, *Woodmyth & Fable* (New York: The Century Company, 1905), 78.

into the water. Add three of your favorite herbs. Place the container outside somewhere where it will receive plenty of sunlight. Leave it there for three days, and then dab a small amount of the liquid onto your eyelids and around your eyes just before dawn or dusk. Walk around your garden in a casual manner, pausing to admire anything that catches your eye. If you are very lucky, you might see some fairies.

Although you can search for Fairyland, it is much safer to contact fairies through dreams and daydreams, as many people who have entered the world of fairies have failed to return. Sit or lie down beside a tree in a wooded area where you are not likely to be disturbed. Close your eyes and take three slow, deep breaths. Allow all the muscles of your body to relax. If you feel completely safe in this environment you can keep your eyes closed. However, if you are in a public park it might be better to daydream with your eyes open.

Start thinking about the fairies and other nature spirits. If your eyes are open, look around and focus on a flower or leaf that is close to you. If your eyes are closed, imagine the most beautiful flower you have ever seen. I used to imagine a pink rose, but I recently switched to orchids.

Allow yourself to daydream about fairies. There is no need to try hard. Let your mind roam freely. If you find it has wandered off and is thinking about something else, gently bring it back by thinking of your desire to communicate with fairies.

After a while, you may start receiving messages from the fairy kingdom in your mind. Remain as still as possible and see what comes to you. You will discover that you can communicate with the fairies telepathically and direct the conversation anywhere you want it to go. Be careful, though. Fairies can be mischievous and may not always be truthful. Thank them for looking after the natural world. Say goodbye to the fairies when you've finished the conversation and allow yourself thirty to sixty seconds to fully return to your everyday world.

If you have a garden, or even a potted plant, you can attract fairies by showering your plants with love and attention. This will attract fairies to your garden. Start talking to the fairies about your plants and thank them for looking after them for you. Describe the beautiful colors, the condition, growth, and anything else you can think of to say about your plants. The fairies will respond by encouraging the plants' growth. The vivid colors of the flowers will become increasingly beautiful as the fairies respond to your efforts. Ask the fairies for suggestions about what you can do to help your plants thrive. Treat every plant in your garden with kindness. This applies even to weeds. When you pull out a weed, do it gently and recycle the weed as compost, so that it is not wasted.

If you leave your home for any period of time, tell the nature spirits what you will be doing and let them know when you'll be back. As soon as possible after returning home, go into your garden and let them know you've returned. You might feel tired after your travels, but you will feel revitalized as soon as you've conversed with the spirits in your garden.

Nature spirits are happiest in places that are treated with love, respect, and reverence. We will discuss how to create a nature grove in the next chapter.

thirteen

Creating a Nature Grove

*G*ardens have always been considered sacred places. The Garden of Eden is considered a form of paradise. Jesus spent his last night in a garden, and Mary Magdalene spoke to him some days later, again in a garden. In fact, on that occasion she thought he was a gardener. The ancient Greeks loved their gardens, and enjoyed spending quiet times in them communing with nature. Philosophers such as Epicurus (341–270 BCE) taught their students in gardens because the quiet, peaceful, and spiritual environment helped concentration and learning.

You can commune with flowers, trees, and all of nature whenever you wish, by seeking out a suitable place. If you live in a city apartment, you might have to visit a park or nature reserve. If you live in the country, or have your own garden, you might be able to commune with nature whenever you go outdoors. Indoor potted plants can suffice as well, especially when the weather is bad.

Everyone needs contact with nature. Going for a walk in the woods or beside a lake enables us to put things into perspective, and discover what is really important in life. You should take your time when communing with nature. Watch the flight of birds, the shadows created by trees, the industry of bees, and the colors of the different plants. You may return home with nothing but a pebble, but in reality you will be carrying in your heart and soul a priceless treasure that will nourish every part of your being.

Many people find it helpful to have their own special place they can visit whenever they wish. Spending time in your own nature grove can be a spiritual experience. It always restores body, mind, and soul. In addition to this, you will find your sacred space ideal for performing spells, divination, and magic.

The size and layout of your nature grove are entirely up to you. I have friends who have a tiny backyard that they have transformed into an oasis of peace and beauty. Farmers we know have transformed an area of bush into an attractive place they can visit whenever they seek tranquility and spiritual growth. The size of a nature grove is not important.

I spoke to someone yesterday who has turned part of her yard into a "fairy grotto." It contains statues of fairies, gnomes, and toadstools. She has hung colored glass from the branches of the trees and has established a small vegetable garden in the middle. This woman originally did this to please her four-year-old daughter, but she is now convinced that her fairy grotto has attracted devas and other nature spirits, as everything grows magnificently and without effort in this corner of her garden. Not surprisingly, her fairy grotto is gradually expanding in size.

Recently I visited the home of someone who has created an entirely different nature grove in her property. She has created a Japanese garden in a sheltered, private part of her property. She immediately feels relaxed whenever she spends time in it. She even feels relaxed when she thinks about her Japanese garden while she's away from home.

Your nature grove might not even be on your own property. You could find an attractive corner of a park that you can use. It doesn't matter if people walk through it while you are there. In fact, you will scarcely notice them.

You can make your nature grove sacred purely by your presence. As you spend quiet times in your designated space, you will gradually imbue it with your spiritual energy. As a result, this area will become more and more special and sacred to you as time goes on.

You can speed up the process by conducting a ceremony in your special space. You might smudge the area with sweet herbs. You might sing songs or beat a drum to welcome angels, fairies, and nature spirits to your nature grove. You might conduct a special ceremony during which you eat cake and drink wine. You might burn a candle and perform a divination in front of it. You might create an altar and pray, meditate, or conduct a ritual in front of it. You can choose, one, two, or even all of the above ideas in order to make your special space more sacred.

Smudging

People have burned herbs and spices for thousands of years to cleanse and purify people, objects, rooms, and outdoor areas. This is a powerful and magical exercise. The scent of the herbs stimulates the senses, and the sight of the sweet-smelling smoke drifting heavenward serves as a reminder that you are creating a sacred space.

You can use whatever herbs you wish. Sage is probably the herb most commonly used for smudging in the United States, and you might want to add cedar, juniper, and sweetgrass to it. In the United Kingdom, you might want to experiment with lavender, mugwort, and rosemary. The herbs can be burned singly or as a mixture.

Herbs can become extremely hot when burned. Be careful, and make sure to use a fireproof container. Once the herbs are burning, use a fan or feather to spread the smoke. It is not a good idea to blow the herbs, as any negativity you may have in your body will be spread into the herbs.

A good alternative to burning the herbs in a container is to make or obtain a smudge stick. This is a bundle of herbs, slightly larger in size than a carrot and held together with cotton thread. The advantage of a smudge stick is that you can move around with it and smudge the perimeter of your sacred space.

Singing and Drumming

Sound is another effective way to consecrate your sacred space. Shamans traditionally perform rhythmic drumming, but you can play any instrument you wish. Rattles, bells, and cymbals are possibilities. A friend of mine uses his guitar. Singing works well, and it makes no difference if you can or cannot sing in tune. You may choose to sing a favorite song. Alternatively, you might like to sing different sounds as they occur to you. Anything that feels right for you will work.

Nowadays you can also play CDs, but I prefer to create my own sound rather than listening to someone else's music. The only possible exception to that is a drumming CD. There are a number of good ones available.

March or dance around the perimeter of your sacred space, singing or playing your instrument. Continue doing this until you feel tired. Rest in the center of your space until you have recovered. Repeat if desired.

Ritual

I always enjoy performing rituals in my sacred space. I treat the sacred space as a magic circle. Before starting, I place some special objects in the center of the circle, on the ground or on my altar if I have one. The objects are a wand to symbolize the fire element, a miniature sword (air), a silver dish inscribed with a pentacle (earth), and a wine glass containing wine (water). The pentacle also serves as a plate and contains a slice of fruitcake. Sometimes I use a candle instead of a wand to symbolize the fire element.

I then leave the circle, and start again. I enter the circle and face east. I close my eyes and visualize Archangel Raphael. I welcome him as soon as I sense that he is present. I turn to the south, visualizing and then welcoming Archangel Michael. I repeat this with Archangel Gabriel in the west and Archangel Uriel in the north. This provides me, and my sacred space, with symbolic protection. I thank the archangels for looking after me and my sacred space.

My ritual continues with the objects that symbolize the four elements. I face the east and hold the sword high in the air (the air element relates to the east). I turn to the south and hold the wand as high as I can (the fire element relates to the south). I turn to the west and hold the wine glass high in the air (the water element relates to the west). Finally, I face north and hold the pentacle between my cupped hands (the earth element relates to north). Once I have done this, I walk around the perimeter of my sacred space in a clockwise direction. Next, I eat part of the cake and drink some of the wine.

Now I thank the universal life force for enabling me to create a sacred space, and I invite angels, fairies, and nature spirits to enter the space whenever they wish. Once I have done this, I can continue with the ritual in any way I choose. This might include magic or a divination. I might simply spend time absorbing the energies of the plant life around me.

I finish the ritual by walking around the perimeter of my space in a counterclockwise direction. I then face east and formally thank Archangel Raphael for his assistance. I continue by facing south and thanking Archangel Michael. I then thank Gabriel and Uriel.

I crumble the remaining cake and empty the wine glass onto the ground. This symbolically feeds the nature spirits. The ritual is now ended. I leave the circle, leaving behind the objects I brought into it.

It is a good idea to relax for a while after conducting a ritual. Eat and drink something, and think about the ritual. When you feel ready, gather up the objects you used in the ritual and leave.

This is a very simple example of a ritual. You can dress it up as much as you wish. You might want to wear special robes while performing your rituals. You might want to light candles and/or burn incense. You might like to sprinkle water for purification around your magic circle before starting the ritual. You may want to start your ritual by ringing a bell or banging a gong. It is a good idea to bathe before conducting a ritual. However, this may not be possible, especially if your space is a long way from home.

There is no right or wrong way to perform a ritual. What is important is your intent. You can conduct rituals inside your sacred space as often as you wish. Obviously, there must be a purpose for each ritual, and this is decided ahead of time. How you conduct each ritual will depend on the purpose you have selected.

Divination

Your sacred space will become extremely useful if you work with tarot cards, rune stones, or any other divination system. I prefer to perform divinations for myself in my sacred space, but there is no reason why you can't divine for others here as well if you wish. You will discover that added insights will come to you when you work inside your sacred space.

Again, you can window-dress your divinations as much as you like. I usually light a candle. A good friend of mine likes to have New Age music playing in the background. She also displays bronze figurines of different gods and goddesses she has collected over the years. Sometimes she creates a circle of crystals inside her sacred space, which she works inside.

Altar

An altar is a sacred object in itself. It should be treated with respect at all times. You should not kneel or step onto your altar, as this is considered disrespectful. An altar can be useful in many ways. It provides a place to hold the different objects you will be using in your rituals. It gives you a flat surface to work on. It is a place of spiritual focus.

Your altar should be placed in the middle of your sacred space. I like to face east when working on my altar. Some people prefer facing north. You will need to experiment to decide which direction you feel works best for you.

The altar can be made from anything. I have used a sawed-off tree trunk as an altar. I often use a card table because it can be carried easily. An acquaintance of mine is extremely fortunate as he has a large flat-surfaced rock in the middle of his sacred space. Many people use a square of cloth that they lay on the ground as an altar. I prefer to use a table myself, since I like to work standing rather than kneeling and I like a flat surface to work on.

It is important that your altar is used solely for spiritual purposes. My card-table altar would lose all its power if I also used it when playing cards, or if I kept it as a place to store gardening tools or other items.

You should make your altar look as pleasing as possible. I have several special tablecloths that I use to cover my altar. Again, they are not used for any other purpose.

In addition to the objects that you need for your rituals, decorate your altar with objects that have special meaning for you. These might include candles, photographs, icons, ornaments, or anything else that feels spiritual to you.

Look after your altar when it is not being used. I have a large cloth bag to protect my card table, for instance. Your altar should be cleaned regularly. I smudge my altar every now and again, too.

Spells

Traditionally, a spell is a word or phrase that is believed to possess magical power when spoken or written during a magical ritual. Spells have always played an integral role in the world of magic and can be cast for good or ill. A good spell is called a blessing. An evil spell is known as a hex. A curse is a good example of an evil spell. The intent of the person performing the spell determines whether it is good or bad. You must be very brave or extremely foolish to cast an evil spell, though, as in magic everything you send out comes back to you threefold. Consequently, it's extremely important that you only ever perform white, or good, magic. It is possible to inadvertently perform a bad spell. You can use a spell to attract a partner, for instance, but you can't perform a spell to attract a specific person to you. This is black magic, as you are ignoring the needs of the other person. Spells need to be performed for the good of everyone involved.

The words are usually spoken or visualized while the magician performs the ritual. Spells can be cast for many purposes, including fertility, forgiveness, good fortune, happiness, healing, longevity, love, money, psychic protection, and success.

Ahead of time, write down the spell you desire. In a spell for psychic protection, you might write: "I desire psychic protection because I am becoming exhausted and overwhelmed with the stresses of life."

Start with a normal ritual, along the lines of the one described above. Once you have welcomed the universal life force, sit or lie down in the center of your circle. Write your spell down again and read it several times, preferably out loud, using as much energy and volume as you can. Close your eyes and allow every part of your body to relax. Think of the plants inside your sacred space and allow yourself to absorb their positive energies. Visualize individual plants in your mind, and feel their love and inspiration. Continue this for as long as possible. Sooner or later, your mind will start to wander. When you reach this stage, recite the spell again. Repeat it several times if possible. Slowly count from one to five and open your eyes.

Conclude the ritual and leave your sacred space. There is no need to think any more about the spell. You have sent it out into the universe, and you will start noticing the benefits of it immediately.

Prayer

Prayer is a spiritual communication with the divine. Clement of Alexandria (c.150–c.215), an early Christian father, said: "Prayer is a conversation with God." You can pray anywhere you happen to be, at any time. It makes no difference if you belong to an orthodox religion, or none. Many people find it helpful to pray inside their sacred spaces. I like to use prayer as the central part of my ritual. It is natural to start praying after welcoming the universal life force. Once my prayers are concluded, I then complete the ritual.

However, I have spoken to many people who use their sacred space as a place of prayer but prefer not to include it in a ritual. They like to sit down comfortably in their sacred space, close their eyes, and immediately pray. In my experience, both methods work equally well.

Creative Visualization

Your sacred space is also a good place to perform creative visualizations. Creative visualization is the art of deliberately using your imagination to create whatever it is you desire. Every time you daydream you are visualizing. However, these daydreams are random and not directed at a specific outcome.

Creative visualization can be used for many different purposes. Naturally, you should visualize positive outcomes. You might visualize world peace, for example. You might visualize something that you want for yourself, such as a new car or house.

Most people who have achieved greatness in their lives became that way by visualizing their success before it was achieved. Many of these people were called dreamers. The people who called them that obviously had no idea how powerful daydreams can be. A creative visualization is, in essence, a guided daydream.

Spend time in your sacred space and think about what you most desire. I like to lie down and close my eyes when doing this. I find myself becoming distracted too easily if I have my eyes open. However, most people daydream with their eyes open, and you may find you prefer to do it that way. Focus on your desire. You might want to improve your health, progress in your career, eliminate a negative habit, or achieve a specific goal. It makes no difference what it is you desire. In your mind, visualize yourself and your life once you have achieved your goal. Allow the feelings of this success to reach every part of your body, mind, and spirit. Focus on your goal for as long as you can before returning to your everyday life. Continue doing these visualizations as frequently as possible until you have achieved your desire.

By doing this, you are focusing on what you most desire rather than what you wish to avoid. Focusing your attention on what you want encourages your mind to start working on your goal, and new ideas and opportunities will open up for you. Obviously, you need to evaluate them and seize the right opportunities. Creative visualization is the vital first step to success. However, it is not magic. Hard work is also required to make your dreams come true.

Creative visualizing could be described as conscious dreaming. We all dream unconsciously, too, every time we go to sleep. Dreaming about plants is the subject of the next chapter.

fourteen

Plant Dreams

*P*eople have always been fascinated with their dreams. The ancient Babylonians believed dreams were sent by malign spirits. The Egyptians believed dreams came from the gods, and they used their dreams to ask for help and guidance.

The Greeks also considered dreams to be messages from the gods and asked Asclepius, the god of healing, to intercede on their behalf. There were hundreds of temples dedicated to Asclepius scattered throughout Greece. The most famous of these was at Epidaurus. In some respects, these temples were like health spas, as the patients there adhered to a special diet, performed specific exercises, and took special baths. However, the most important part of the treatment was the sacred dreaming. The patients slept in a dormitory, and in their dreams received a visit from Asclepius or one of his priests. The patients awoke in the morning and returned home cured. Records were kept of the many cures, and there is no evidence of any failures or deaths.[32] The temples devoted to Asclepius also contained sacred snakes, and he was often depicted holding a staff with a serpent intertwined around it. This is the source of the medical symbol of two snakes entwined around a staff.

Almost three thousand years ago, Homer (c. ninth century BCE), the great Greek poet, wrote about dreams and their interpretation. In the first book of the Bible, Joseph interpreted the pharaoh's dream about seven fat cows and seven lean cows (Genesis 41:17–28).

The Taoist philosopher Chuang-tzu (fourth century BCE) described the experience of waking up and being unable to determine which was reality: his life awake or his dream life. On one occasion he dreamt he was a butterfly, flying gently from place to place. When he woke up, he lay in bed trying to determine if he was a man dreaming he was a butterfly, or a butterfly dreaming he was a man.

---

32. *The New Encyclopaedia Britannica*, Macropaedia, volume 11 (Chicago: Encyclopaedia Britannica, 15th edition, 1983), 826.

Many creative people have made constructive use of their dreams. The words to Samuel Taylor Coleridge's (1772–1834) famous poem, *Kubla Khan* (1797), came to him in a dream. He was writing them down when he was interrupted, and the rest of the poem vanished from his mind. Mary Shelley (1797–1851) dreamed the story of *Frankenstein, or the Modern Prometheus*. The dream terrified her, and she rightly believed it would have the same effect on her readers. The story of *Dr. Jekyll and Mr. Hyde* came to Robert Louis Stevenson (1850–1894) in a dream. Many of the poems of William Butler Yeats (1865–1939) were inspired by his dreams. More recently, the melody of the song "Yesterday" is believed to have come to Paul McCartney in a dream.[33]

We all dream. Researchers have proved this by waking volunteers at different times during the night to ask them if they were dreaming. Most people forget their dreams as soon as they wake up. Fortunately, it is possible to remember your dreams.

The method I find most helpful is to write down everything I can remember about my dreams as soon as I wake up. Partially forgotten details frequently come back as I'm writing. If you wake up knowing that you've just had a dream but cannot remember it, remain in the same position you were in when you woke up and try to keep your mind and body relaxed. Often, details of the dream will return to you when you do this. There is no need to worry if the memories do not return. If the dream is important to you, you will dream it again.

There are different types of dreams. Everyday dreams show your mind is evaluating and working on events that are going on in your life. Usually, they have little significance but can indicate when changes are about to occur.

Much more important are symbolic dreams. These contain more power and emotion than an everyday dream. The occurrences

---

33. Richard Craze, *The Dictionary of Dreams and their Meanings* (London: Hermes House, 2003), 89.

in the dream are seldom logical, and the scenes and people you meet in the dream are likely to be unfamiliar. Plants appear frequently in symbolic dreams.

Dreams of desire contain elements that we wish to have in our own lives. For instance, if you want to have a baby but have not conceived yet, you might dream of nursing and looking after your own baby. Someone recently told me of his dream in which he broke a world record and won an important race. He is a good athlete, but is not—at least not yet—a world-class athlete. His dream was obviously a dream of desire. Hopefully, it will motivate him to make his dream a reality.

Recurring dreams are dreams that are repeated many times, usually with very little change in theme or content. There is always a lesson to be learned from recurring dreams, and they need to be evaluated carefully to discover what the lesson may be.

There are many examples of prophetic dreams. Abraham Lincoln (1809–1865) dreamt of his own funeral a few days before he was assassinated. Caligula also dreamt of his assassination the night before he was murdered. The best-known examples of prophetic dreams are those that are publicized, usually because they involve world events or people in leadership roles. However, many people experience prophetic dreams relating to themselves and their loved ones. Often these people do not recognize their dream as being prophetic until after the actual event has taken place. That is why it is useful to keep a dream diary, so the dream is recorded and not forgotten.

Nightmares give you an opportunity to deal with old fears. If you wake up after experiencing a nightmare, write down all the details you can remember before returning to sleep. You will find your fears and anxieties will dissipate as you do this. Nightmares should never be taken literally. They are always fantasies constructed around a particular fear.

Plants can figure in every type of dream, but they are most often recognized in symbolic dreams. Some of these—especially phallic symbols like asparagus, bananas, carrots, cucumbers, and even trees—are likely to be obvious. However, most are subtler than this. Plant symbolism is likely to be present but unnoticed in other dreams. While writing in your dream diary, it is worth asking yourself if you remember anything about the flowers and trees that may have been in the dream you are recording.

Flowers are usually positive dream symbols, as they represent beauty, hope, innocence, safety, security, and happiness. To dream of a field of wild flowers, for instance, reveals a yearning for freedom and wide-open spaces. Dreaming of a garden shows that you are loved and respected by others. You can expect a pleasant surprise if you dream that you are picking flowers from a beautiful garden. If your dream includes a basket of flowers you can expect a wedding or a birth in the family. You must seize a valuable opportunity if your dream involves smelling flowers. It is a sign of hope if the flowers are in bud. If they are in full flower, it is a sign of fulfillment, beauty, and happiness. Dying or withered blooms are an indication of sadness, loathing, and the death of cherished hopes.

In dreams, trees usually resemble some aspect of your makeup. This might be your past, present, or future—or perhaps your physical, mental, or spiritual growth. A young, healthy tree indicates youth, enthusiasm, energy, and positivity. Dreaming of evergreen trees is a sign that you will remain forever young inside. Older trees suggest stability and conservatism. Dying or dead trees represent old age and death.

The four seasons also reveal the different stages of life. A tree covered with blossoms or buds symbolizes fertility and youth. Rich summer foliage symbolizes the prime of life. Autumn leaves symbolize middle age. The bare branches of winter symbolize old age.

Blossoms on trees are always a positive symbol. They indicate youth, happiness, and frivolity. They can also indicate that a relationship is "blossoming." Acorns sometimes symbolize pregnancy or the birth of a new idea.

Groups of trees, such as a grove, wood or forest, symbolize a community you belong to. This might indicate your colleagues at work, the neighborhood you live in, your town, city, or even country.

Trunks of dead trees can symbolize your ancestors and people you loved who are now dead.

Like all living things, plants go through a process of growth and decay. Consequently, plants are often a symbol of growth and change. Cultivated plants show you have potential that should be cultivated and nurtured. Decaying flowers reveal that you have attained everything possible from a particular situation. Wild flowers indicate that at least part of you desires freedom.

Colorful flowers in full bloom symbolize optimism and hope. Dead or dying flowers are a sign of disappointment and sadness. Winter trees also symbolize sadness, and a time to withdraw and make plans for a better future.

It is a positive sign to receive a bouquet of flowers in your dream. This is a sign of approval, acceptance, achievement, honor, and respect.

Flowers blooming in a barren landscape show that your sense of optimism and positivity will enable you to overcome any hurdles, and that you will ultimately achieve your goals.

Flowers often symbolize the feminine side of a person's makeup. The person may conceal this side of their character during waking hours but is unable to deny it in the world of dreams.

Weeds symbolize negativity. Weeds can overpower your garden and ultimately destroy it. They are a sign that you should focus on the positive aspects of your life rather than the negative.

Vegetables take time to grow and mature. Dreaming of them is a sign that you need to persevere to succeed. If you do this, you will achieve your goals despite difficulties and hardship along the way. Ideally, you will dream of healthy vegetables. Dreaming of sick or unhealthy vegetables is a sign of poverty and lack in your life. The shape of many vegetables suggests sexuality, and the context of the dream will tell you if this is, or is not, the case.

Many fruits are associated with sexuality, too. If a man finds himself dreaming of bananas, he should evaluate their condition. A green, unripe banana symbolizes sexual immaturity, while a ripe, yellow banana symbolizes sexual maturity. Sadly, dreaming of an overripe, brownish banana shows his sexual peak is in the past. Curvaceous fruits such as melons are associated with breasts, and women dreaming of them need to evaluate them in the same way as men do with phallic-shaped fruit. Seed-filled fruits such as pomegranates and figs are related to fruitfulness and pregnancy. The pineapple has always been associated with fertility, too.

Of course, fruit does not always relate to sex. Dreaming of a bowl of fruit is a sign that life is bountiful and pleasant. An orange can indicate a sunny future, while a lemon could indicate something sour is about to occur.

Dreaming that you are gardening shows that you are concerned with the practical aspects of life. If you are digging or hoeing, it is a sign that you are making plans and preparing the groundwork of a venture. If you are planting in your dream, it is a sign that you are creating new opportunities. Harvesting is a sign that you are reaping the rewards of your endeavors. Dreaming that you are mowing the lawn is a sign that you are doing important work as far as maintenance and repair is concerned.

In dream lore, it is considered beneficial to dream of certain plants:

Almond

Dreaming of almonds is a sign of an upcoming journey. Sweet almonds reveal that it will be a worthwhile and prosperous trip. If the almonds taste bitter, the outcome will be less than you had hoped.

Apple

It is a highly positive sign to dream of apples. They signify success in all undertakings, a happy marriage, and a long life. Bright red apples symbolize fertility, and promise a large and healthy family. Because of its associations with Adam and Eve, a bright red apple can also symbolize seductiveness. Golden apples signify a desire for fame, and green apples symbolize wealth. Dreaming of stealing apples is not a good sign, as it shows you are trying to steal someone else's lover.

Apricot

Dreaming of apricots is highly positive. They indicate good health and happiness. If you are single, dreaming of apricots means your future partner is not far away.

Buttercup

Dreaming of buttercups indicates that your finances are about to improve, as long as you are prepared to do whatever work is necessary.

Carnation

Dreaming of carnations indicates the possibility of a passionate love affair. You need to think carefully before deciding whether to seize or decline this opportunity.

Carrot

Dreaming of carrots is a sign of financial success. It is also a sign of a positive outcome if you are involved in any form of litigation.

Chrysanthemum

Dreaming of yellow chrysanthemums is a positive sign, as it indicates true love. White chrysanthemums are not a good sign, though, as they reveal your lover may be about to leave. In Eastern belief, chrysanthemums are a symbol of longevity.

Clover

Dreaming of clover signifies good health, happiness, a good marriage, and ultimate prosperity.

Corn

Dreaming of corn can be either a good or bad omen. It is a sign of success to dream that you are picking ripe corn. However, it is a sign of loss if the corn is blighted or damaged in any other way.

Crocus

Dreaming of crocus is a sign of potential danger. You need to be cautious in all love relationships.

Cucumber

It is highly positive for an invalid to dream of a cucumber, as this is a sign of recovery and a return to good health. It is also a sign of success in business and the possibility of a happy overseas vacation.

Currant

It is a good sign to dream of currants. It promises wealth, happiness, and many friends.

Daffodil

Daffodils indicate a reconciliation with a former friend. Past events will be forgotten, and you'll be able to continue the friendship as if nothing had happened.

Daisy

It is a good omen to dream of daisies in spring or summer, as they bring luck into your life. However, it is considered bad luck to dream of them in the autumn.

Dandelion

Children enjoy trying to blow away all of a dandelion's seeds in one puff, while making a wish. It is a sign you have a secret wish or desire if you find yourself holding a dandelion in your dream.

Fig

It is a good sign to dream of figs or fig trees. They promise health, wealth, and long-lasting relationships. They also indicate a healthy and contented old age. Figs are also a sign of fertility and pregnancy. Consequently, the nature of the dream needs to be evaluated to determine the correct symbology of the fig in each case.

Forget-me-not

Dreaming of forget-me-nots indicates that your partner is unable to satisfy all your needs. You will need to discuss matters with your partner to see what can, and what cannot, be resolved.

Forsythia

Forsythia is a positive flower, and dreaming of it reveals that you are enthusiastic and glad to be alive.

Foxglove

The beautiful foxglove contains digitalin, which is used to treat people with heart problems. Dreaming of a foxglove can indicate either a broken heart or a need to see a doctor.

Garlic

Dreaming of garlic has meaning for men but not for women. It is extremely lucky for a man to dream that he has garlic in his home. However, it is a sign of domestic difficulties if he dreams that he is eating garlic.

Grass

It is usually a positive sign to dream of grass. Healthy, green grass signifies a long and happy life, and a comfortable old age. If the grass is withered or dying, it is a sign of sickness and ill health.

Hazelnut

You will discover a hidden treasure if you find hazelnuts in your dreams. This treasure may not be jewelry or gold but may well be a serendipitous discovery or chance encounter. Eating hazelnuts in your dreams signifies considerable prosperity.

Honeysuckle

Dreaming of honeysuckle shows there will be tears, which will quickly be replaced by smiles and laughter.

Iris

Dreaming of irises shows that you will shortly hear good news relating to you or a close family member.

Ivy

Ivy is one of the most propitious plants to dream about. It promises good friends, great happiness, and financial success.

Jasmine

It is a fortunate sign to dream of jasmine. This is an extremely good omen for people in love.

Lilac

Dreaming of lilacs is usually a sign of good luck in love and romance. This ultimately makes for a long and happy marriage. The exception to this is to dream of purple lilacs, as this indicates a misfortune ahead.

Lily

Dreaming of lilies in season is a sign of an upcoming marriage, one that will be long-lasting and happy. Lilies frequently indicate the start of a spiritual awakening. Dreaming of lilies out of season is a sign of frustration. Dreaming of withered or dead lilies is a sign of a severe illness.

Marigold

Dreaming of marigolds portends success, happiness, and prosperity. It is extremely fortunate for young lovers to dream of marigolds.

Mistletoe

Dreaming of mistletoe is a sign of possible temptation. To avoid future difficulties you should remain true to your partner.

Mushroom

Dreaming of mushrooms is a sign of a small, pleasant surprise. However, it can also indicate that you are being kept in the dark about something important. Dreaming of hallucinogenic mushrooms is a sign that you need more magic or fun in your life.

Myrtle

Dreaming of myrtle is a sign of more than one marriage. Dreaming of myrtle on more than one occasion indicates that your second partner will also have been married before.

Oak

Dreaming of oak trees usually indicates a long, happy, productive life. If the oak tree also bears acorns, you will become wealthy. A healthy, thriving oak tree indicates children who will bring honor to the family.

Olive

It is a positive sign to dream of an olive tree, as it symbolizes peace and prosperity. Dreaming of an olive branch is a sign that some difficulty is coming to an end.

Palm

Dreaming of a palm tree is a sign that you need a good vacation, preferably one in an exotic location. The palm tree was a symbol of victory in Roman times. Consequently, dreaming of a palm tree sometimes indicates that a major success is about to occur.

Peach

Dreaming of peaches signifies pleasure, luxury, indulgence, happiness, and good health.

Peony

Dreaming of peonies indicates that you have been, or shortly will be, presented with an opportunity. You should evaluate it carefully and seize it if it seems promising.

Pomegranate

Dreaming of pomegranates is a sign of success in all areas of life. It means a good relationship to someone seeking a partner, better health to someone who is ill, and prosperity to someone engaged in business.

Poppy

Because opium can be produced from their seeds, poppies have symbolized sleep and death since at least the time of the ancient Greeks. However, symbology can change. Since the First World War poppies have come to symbolize remembrance. This is because they were flowering in the battlefields of northern France when hundreds of thousands of young men were killed in battle.

Primrose

Dreaming of primroses shows that you are about to make a new friend, and both of you will find joy and happiness in this friendship.

Quince

Dreaming of quinces is a sign of improving health and physical fitness. Other minor problems and concerns will soon be resolved.

Raspberry

Dreaming of raspberries indicates good news from someone overseas. It also indicates a successful marriage and healthy children. Raspberries are hardy plants, and dreaming of them can also indicate success as a result of hard work.

Rose

This is the best plant of all to dream about, as long as the roses are healthy. A red rose indicates true love, successful relationships, good health, and ultimate prosperity. It can also indicate a wedding. However, if the roses are dead or dying, the outcome is losses and disappointment. A white rose is a symbol of purity. Dreaming of a pink rose indicates a romance. It is bad luck to dream of a black rose, as this indicates death.

If you dream of a dozen red roses, it is a sign of a long-lasting, passionate relationship.

Dreaming of roses in bud is a sign of innocence and virginity.

Snowdrop

Dreaming of a snowdrop is a sign that you have unresolved problems. You should confide in someone you trust, and the difficulties will quickly disappear.

Sycamore

It is a sign of marriage if a single person dreams of a sycamore. A married person who dreams of a sycamore needs to avoid jealousy.

Thistle

It is a sign of unexpected good luck to dream of a thistle. Something pleasant is about to occur.

Vine

Dreaming of vines is a sign of health, fertility, and prosperity. This is a good time to make plans for expansion and progress.

Violet

Dreaming of violets is a sign that you are about to progress in an important area of your life. This means your circumstances will improve. It is an indication that planning and hard work are starting to pay off. Violets are also a sign of affection. Dreaming of violets can also be a sign that you will marry someone younger than you.

Wallflower

Wallflowers are a positive symbol to dream about. They tell a lover that their partner is true. They reveal to someone who is sick that good health is not far away. If a single person dreams of a bouquet of wallflowers, it is a sign that a proposal is imminent.

• • •

Most of this book has been concerned with flowers and trees in the Western world. However, the East also has a rich history and folklore concerning flowers and trees. We will look at magic plants in the East in the next chapter.

fifteen

Spiritual and Magical Plants in the East

here are five elements in Taoist philosophy: wood, fire, earth, metal, and water. The wood element relates to plants. It also relates to the direction east, the color green, spring, wisdom, and immortality. The fact that plants and wisdom are connected in this way shows the powerful effect plants have on the physical, mental, emotional, and spiritual well-being of humanity. Plants are not simply objects of beauty and a source of food. They are essential for happiness, peace of mind, and life itself.

All human and animal life ultimately depends on plants for survival. Any major changes in an environment that affect plant life will inevitably affect humans and animals as well. The clearing of forests, for instance, can cause floods, droughts, and other disasters.

Plants also taught the ancient philosophers the value of timing. The philosophers watched the changing seasons and discovered that it is impossible to change nature. The Taoists devised a sixty-year cyclic system, known as the Ganzhi system, that predicts the various combinations of time and the environment. The Chinese also divide the year into twenty-four periods, as well as the four seasons. All of these are used to make predictions in the annual Chinese almanac.

Each of the four seasons has a flower to symbolize the period: peony symbolizes spring; lotus symbolizes summer; chrysanthemum, autumn; and plum blossom, winter. Another grouping associates bamboo with spring, the orchid or iris with summer, the chrysanthemum with autumn, and the plum blossom with winter. This second arrangement is called "the four gentlemen" because it comprises four valuable qualities frequently depicted by Chinese artists. The bamboo symbolizes endurance; the orchid or iris, warmth; the chrysanthemum, integrity; and the plum blossom, nobility. The bamboo, pine, and plum are known as the "three friends." They demonstrate endurance by thriving and growing during winter. Together they symbolize enduring friendship.

Each month of the year is also symbolized by a plant: prunus (plum), peach, peony, cherry, magnolia, pomegranate, lotus, pear, mallow, chrysanthemum, gardenia, and poppy.[34] In the Chinese lunar calendar some months have twenty-nine days and others have thirty. Because the lunar twelve months do not complete a solar year, an additional month is added every third year. The Chinese New Year is held annually on a day between January 21st and February 19th. The eighth day after New Year is considered the birthday of rice and cereals. Fruit and vegetables are celebrated on the ninth day, and corn and barley on the tenth. If the weather is fine on their birthdays, the crops they produce that year are believed to be plentiful.

Every woman is represented by a flower or tree in the other world. The Festival of Flowers, held on the twelfth day of the second moon, commemorates this. Women and children hang red papers on flowers, shrubs, and trees, and then praise the plants. This assures a bountiful harvest.

Chinese herbal medicine has been practiced for thousands of years, and uses the five elements and the yin-yang principle of opposites to affect a cure. Tea was introduced to China from India in the sixth century. It was originally drunk for medicinal purposes and became a popular drink during the Tang dynasty (618–907 CE). It did not reach the West until the end of the sixteenth century.

Chinese Plant Meanings

The Chinese have a complex system of symbols. Flowers, in particular, were given positive symbolism intended to motivate and inspire everyone who saw them. Here is a list of the more common meanings:

Apple: female beauty, family wealth, peace
Apricot: female beauty, fertility
Azalea: female beauty
Bamboo: filial piety, nobility, modesty, youth, longevity

---

34. C. A. S. Williams, *Outlines of Chinese Symbolism and Art Motives* (Shanghai: Kelly and Walsh, 1941), 192. (Reprinted by Dover Publications, 1976.)

Banana: self-education, application, discipline

Camellia: nobility, relaxation

Chrysanthemum: high position, comfortable life, autumn, cheerfulness

Convolvulus: love and marriage

Dandelion: protection, good health, money

Geranium: prosperity

Gourd: children

Hibiscus: wealth, honor, fame

Jasmine: charming lady, sweetness, friendship, affection

Loquat: luck

Lotus: fertility, fruitfulness, summer, wealth. The lotus is the sacred flower of China.

Magnolia: "the flower of nocturnal tenderness," charm and sweetness

Mulberry: mother, hard work

Narcissus: marriage, wealth, good fortune

Oak: strength

Oleander: beauty

Olive: education

Orange: wealth

Orchid: fertility, love, perfection, refinement

Palm: happy old age

Peach: marriage

Pear: justice, purity of heart

Peony: affection, love, feminine beauty, wealth, honor. The peony can also attract the right marriage partner.

Persimmon: joy, business success

Pine: endurance

Plum: considerable wealth

Pomegranate: fertility, many children

Willow: female sweetness, meekness

Wisteria: wealth

Magical Trees

Tree worship was practiced in ancient China, and it was rare for a tree standing near a grave or temple to be cut down. In fact, trees were sometimes planted on the grave itself. This enabled the soul of the tree to support and strengthen the soul of the dead person. Pine and cypress trees were especially popular for this purpose because they possessed large amounts of spiritual energy.[35]

Chinese literature is full of stories about trees crying out in anguish when they were cut down. One legend tells the story of Wu-Kang, who was studying to become an Immortal. He was banished to the moon after making too many mistakes in his examinations. He could not return to Earth until he had cut down the cassia tree that grew on the moon. Unfortunately for Wu-Kang, every time he chopped even a sliver off this cassia tree, another sliver grew to replace it. Consequently, he is still there and children call him the Old Man on the Moon. The cassia tree on the moon is still complete and healthy.

Trees were often decorated with garlands and lanterns as a form of tree worship. Strips of red cloth or paper were sometimes attached to trees to protect them, and to ward off evil spirits.

Apple

The Chinese apple tree is actually a crabapple. The apple trees we know in the West are not found in China. Apple blossoms symbolize feminine beauty, as well as peace and tranquility.

Apricot

The apricot tree symbolizes fertility, fruitfulness, and the second month of the Chinese calendar. It is also a symbol of feminine beauty. Apricot kernels symbolize the beauty of Chinese women's eyes.

---

35. Ong Hean-Tatt, *Chinese Plant Symbolisms: A Guide to the Symbolic Value of Plants in Chinese Culture* (Selangor Darul Ehsan, Malaysia: Pelanduk Publications (M) Sdn Bhd, 1999), 164.

Bamboo

The bamboo is a symbol of longevity. It represents modesty, refinement, and because it is hollow, open-mindedness. It also repels negative energies. Bamboo is used for many purposes. The young shoots are eaten. The pulp can be turned into paper, and the adult plant can be used as a building material and to make furniture and other objects. Even today, a great deal of scaffolding in China is constructed from bamboo. Bamboo has always been a popular subject for Chinese artists. Three trees are frequently found together and are known as the "three friends in winter." They are the bamboo, pine, and plum trees.

Camphor

The camphor tree provides enthusiasm and energy for anyone who needs it.

Cassia

The cassia tree symbolizes forgiveness. It is also related to the rabbit that, according to Chinese folklore, lives on the moon. This rabbit makes pills of immortality under the cassia tree that grows on the moon. These pills confer immortality on anyone who eats them.

Cherry

Every part of the cherry tree is used for medicinal purposes. The fruit symbolizes feminine beauty and has strong sexual connotations. The phrase "eating cherries" is a euphemism for "having sexual intercourse."

Cypress

The cypress tree is believed to possess healing qualities. As it is a long-living tree, it also symbolizes longevity. Eating cypress seeds will keep a person strong, healthy, and youthful well into old age. An additional benefit of eating these seeds is that your hearing and vision will improve.

Japonica

The japonica is known as the "love tree" and symbolizes married life. An old legend explains how this association came about. An emperor desired Lady Lo-chu, but she was already happily married. The emperor beheaded her husband and took Lady Lo-chu to one of his castles in the mountains. She committed suicide by throwing herself over a precipice. The emperor refused to have her buried with her husband, but a japonica tree grew from each grave and the branches intertwined, forming one large tree. Two Mandarin ducks made their home under the tree, creating a perfect symbol of marital bliss.

Mulberry

The mulberry tree is cultivated extensively in China, as the leaves provide food for silkworms. A staff made of mulberry used to be carried by family members who were mourning the death of their mother. The mulberry symbolizes hard work and dedication. It also symbolizes the pleasures and satisfactions of home life. However, it should not be planted in front of a home because it also attracts sorrow.

Orange

The orange symbolizes good fortune, happiness, prosperity, and abundance. The Chinese word for orange is *kum*, which sounds like the word for "gold." It is fortunate to receive a gift of oranges at New Year, as this is considered a wish for happiness and financial success in the year ahead.

Peach

The Chinese consider the peach to be one of the most magical of all trees. It blossoms in February at the start of the New Year. Consequently, it symbolizes spring, marriage, friendship, and longevity. Peaches are sometimes referred to as "fairy fruit" and the "fruit of the immortals." Peach stones are often carved into the shape of locks and carried by children as lucky charms. Peach trees are feared by evil spirits. Until recently, peach blossoms were placed over the front door of homes to ward off bad luck and negative energies.

Pear

The pear tree symbolizes longevity, as the tree continues to bear fruit even when it is extremely old. The pear tree also symbolizes a benevolent government. This association came about when the Duke of Shao dispensed justice impartially under a wild pear tree some three thousand years ago. Lovers and friends should never share a pear by cutting it in two. This is because the words for "pear" and "separation" are phonetically identical.

Persimmon

The persimmon fruit symbolizes joy and happiness. Persimmon trees were frequently planted in temple gardens, as they are long-living and provide shade.

Pine

The pine tree absorbs divine energy and generously disperses it to humans. The pine tree symbolizes steadfastness, self-discipline, and longevity. It also represents the final years of a long life. In addition to this, the pine tree is a symbol of marital happiness because the pine needles grow in pairs. Old pine trees are particularly venerated. Chinese artists enjoy painting pine trees, partly because of their interesting shapes but mainly because of this symbolism. Along with bamboo and plum, the pine tree is one of the "three friends in winter."

Plum

The plum tree symbolizes youthfulness and vitality. It is a highly auspicious tree in China. Legend says Lao Tzu, the great philosopher, was born under one. Along with bamboo and pine, the plum tree is one of the "three friends in winter." The plum tree is the first tree to blossom in spring. In northern China, where it is extremely cold, the process is helped by growing them in glass houses. The plum tree provides good luck, as the five petals symbolize the five traditional gods of luck.

Willow

The willow symbolizes meekness and springtime. It is also a protective tree, and a willow branch hung over a door will provide the family with good luck and protect them from ghosts and evil demons. The phrase "willow feelings and flower wishes" is a euphemism for sexual desire.

Immortality Plants

The Chinese have many legends concerning magical plants that can confer immortality on humans. One story concerns Emperor Shih Huang-Ti of the Chin dynasty (c. 260 BCE). He is best known for overseeing the building of the Great Wall of China. He was told that many men who died during battles were brought back to life when ravens and crows pushed leaves into their mouths. His wise men told him that the plant that produced these remarkable leaves grew only on the Island of Tsu, a three-peaked island visible only to people who were completely pure in heart. The emperor sent five hundred virgin men and women to the island to bring back the plant. Their ship never returned. This may not be surprising, though, as according to the same legend, the five hundred virgins created the royal family of Japan.

This was one of many attempts to find the fabled plant. Over time, a number of long-living plants became known as immortality plants. The most important are camphor, cassia, cherry, chrysanthemum, cinnamon, cypress, fir, ginseng, mushroom, peach, pear, pine, and plum.

Conclusion

I hope this book has helped you discover some of the magical associations attached to every flower and tree, and I hope you are looking at the wonders of nature with completely different eyes.

Some people enter this magical world quickly and easily. Others, for a variety of reasons, find it more difficult.

Many years ago, a man spoke to me after one of my classes, expressing disbelief in nature spirits. Duncan had established a nature grove in his garden, and everything in it was growing well. However, he had not seen any sign of fairy life in the grove.

"Are the plants in your grove growing better than the other plants in your garden?" I asked.

He nodded his head vigorously. "Much better. I talk to the nature spirits while I'm working."

Duncan suddenly stopped and laughed. "I'm talking to spirits I don't believe in."

I suggested that he stop talking to them for a while to see how the plants fared without the regular conversations. He shook his head no.

"I couldn't do that. What if the fairies are real? I don't want to hurt their feelings."

"In that case, why don't you talk to the fairies in every part of your garden and see what happens?" I asked.

He nodded his head. "I just might try that," he said.

Several months later, Duncan arrived at my front door with a basket of vegetables. "I've never had a better crop," he told me as he presented it to me.

"Are you seeing nature spirits yet?" I asked him.

He frowned. "You know, I think I do. Sometimes I see a glitter of light on a leaf, or a flash in the corner of my eye. When I look again, there's nothing there. I don't think I'm fooling myself." He pointed at the vegetables. "And I can't fool myself that I grew those on my own. Something's helping me. You just have to look at my neighbors' gardens to realize something special is happening in mine. I talk all the time to the spirits, and sometimes they talk back. I wouldn't tell many people this, but thoughts come into my mind about what to plant, and where and when to plant it. It's pretty weird stuff, but look at the result." He indicated his beautiful vegetables with a wave of his hand.

It took Duncan several months to realize and accept he was getting outside help in his garden. Jessica was the complete opposite.

She operates a bed-and-breakfast from her home. All of her customers comment on her magnificent garden, and find it hard to believe she knew nothing about gardening before buying the business three years ago. Some years earlier, she had read an article about Findhorn in Scotland, and decided to call on the nature spirits if she ever had a garden. She assumed, rightly, that they would come to her aid, and her garden thrived from the very start.

Jessica found it easy. Duncan found it more difficult but has gradually come to accept the magical world of plants. Everyone is different.

You might be interested in communicating with trees, divination with flowers, the medical aspects of plants, or simply in gaining a better understanding and a closer connection with nature. No matter what your interest in flower and tree magic may be, I wish you great success.

Suggested Reading

Anderson, Frank J. *An Illustrated History of the Herbals.* New York: Columbia University Press, 1977.

Arber, Agnes. *Herbals: Their Origin and Evolution: A Chapter in the History of Botany, 1470–1670.* Second edition. Cambridge, UK: Cambridge University Press, 1986. (Originally published in 1912.)

Bryan, C. P. *Ancient Egyptian Medicine: The Papyrus Ebers.* London: Geoffrey Bles, 1930. (Reprinted in 1974 by Ares Publishers, Chicago.)

Connolly, Shane. *The Secret Language of Flowers.* New York: Rizzoli International, 2004.

Culpeper, Nicholas. *The Complete Herbal: A Book of Natural Remedies of Ancient Ills.* New York: NTC/Contemporary Publishing, 1998.

Dunn, Olive. *Delights of Floral Language.* Auckland: Random House New Zealand, 1993.

Eberhard, Wolfram (translated by G. L. Campbell). *A Dictionary of Chinese Symbols: Hidden Symbols in Chinese Life and Thought.* London: Routledge & Kegan Paul, 1986. (First published as *Lexicon Chinesischer Symbole* by Eugen Diederichs Verlag, Cologne, Germany, 1983.)

Gerard, John. *The Herbal, or General History of Plants.* New York: Dover, 1975. (Originally published in 1633 as *Herball, or Generall Historie of Plantes.*)

Gunther, Robert. *The Greek Herbal of Dioscorides.* Oxford, UK: Oxford University Press, 1934.

Hageneder, Fred. *The Meaning of Trees: Botany, History, Healing, Lore.* San Francisco: Chronicle Books, 2005.

Harvey, Clare G., and Amanda Cochrane. *The Healing Spirit of Plants: An Illustrated Guide to Plant Spirit Medicine.* New York: Sterling, 1999.

Isaacs, Jennifer. *The Secret Meaning of Flowers.* East Roseville, Australia: Simon & Schuster Australia, 1993.

Laufer, Geraldine Adamich. *Tussie-Mussies: The Victorian Art of Expressing Yourself in the Language of Flowers.* New York: Workman, 1993.

Lucas, Richard. *Nature's Medicines: The Folklore, Romance and Value of Herbal Remedies.* West Nyack, NY: Parker, 1966.

Mann, John. *Murder, Magic, and Medicine.* Oxford, UK: Oxford University Press, 1992.

Maury, Marguerite. *The Secret of Life and Youth.* Saffron Walden, UK: C. W. Daniel and Company, 1989. (Originally published in France as *Le Capital Jeunesse*, 1961.)

Mills, Alice. *Mythology: Myths, Legends, & Fantasies.* Sydney, Australia: Hodder Headline Australia, 2003.

Molyneaux, Brian Leigh, and Piers Vitebsky. *Sacred Earth, Sacred Stones.* San Diego, CA: Laurel Glen, 2001.

Moschini, Lisa B. *Drawing the Line: Art Therapy with the Difficult Client.* New York: Wiley, 2005.

Pogačnik, Marko. *Nature Spirits and Elemental Beings: Working with Intelligence in Nature*. Forres, Scotland: Findhorn Press, 1996. (Originally published in German by Droemer Knaur, 1995.)

Polunin, Miriam. *Healing Foods*. London: Dorling Kindersley, 1997.

Rätsch, Christian (translated by John Baker). *The Dictionary of Sacred and Magical Plants*. Santa Barbara, CA: ABC-CLIO, 1992. (Originally published by Akademische Druck-u. Verlagsanstalt, Graz, Austria, 1988.)

Rohde, E. S. *The Old English Herbals*. London: Longmans, Green, and Company, 1922.

Rose, Carol. *Spirits, Fairies, Gnomes and Goblins*. Denver, CO: ABC-CLIO, Inc., 1996.

Russell, Tony, and Catherine Cutler. *The World Encyclopedia of Trees*. London: Lorenz Books, 2003.

Ryman, Danièle. *Danièle Ryman's Aromatherapy Bible*. London: Judy Piatkus, 1991.

Webster, Richard. *Color Magic for Beginners*. Woodbury, MN: Llewellyn, 2006.

———. *Creative Visualization for Beginners*. Woodbury, MN: Llewellyn, 2005.

———. *Omens, Oghams & Oracles: Divination in the Druiditic Tradition*. St. Paul, MN: Llewellyn, 2002.

———. *Praying with Angels*. Woodbury, MN: Llewellyn, 2007.

Williams, C. A. S. *Outlines of Chinese Symbolism and Art Motives*. Third revised edition. Shanghai: Kelly and Walsh, 1941. (Reprinted by Dover Publications, New York, in 1976.) (Originally published as *Outlines of Chinese Symbolism* by Customs College Press, Peiping, China, 1931.)

Zalewski, C. L. *Herbs in Magic and Alchemy: Techniques from Ancient Herbal Lore*. Bridport, UK: Prism Press, 1990.

Index

Free Magazine

Read unique articles by Llewellyn authors, recommendations by experts, and information on new releases. To receive a **free** copy of Llewellyn's consumer magazine, *New Worlds of Mind & Spirit,* simply call 1-877-NEW-WRLD or visit our website at www.llewellyn.com and click on *New Worlds.*

☾ LLEWELLYN ORDERING INFORMATION

Order Online:
Visit our website at www.llewellyn.com, select your books, and order them on our secure server.

Order by Phone:
- Call toll-free within the U.S. at 1-877-NEW-WRLD (1-877-639-9753). Call toll-free within Canada at 1-866-NEW-WRLD (1-866-639-9753)
- We accept VISA, MasterCard, and American Express

Order by Mail:
Send the full price of your order (MN residents add 7% sales tax) in U.S. funds, plus postage & handling to:

Llewellyn Worldwide
2143 Wooddale Drive, Dept. 978-0-7387-1349-6
Woodbury, MN 55125-2989, U.S.A.

Postage & Handling:
Standard (U.S., Mexico, & Canada). If your order is:
$24.99 and under, add $3.00
$25.00 and over, FREE STANDARD SHIPPING

AK, HI, PR: $15.00 for one book plus $1.00 for each additional book.

International Orders (airmail only):
$16.00 for one book plus $3.00 for each additional book

Orders are processed within 2 business days.
Please allow for normal shipping time. Postage and handling rates subject to change.

Color Magic For Beginners

RICHARD WEBSTER

From our clothes to the color of our bedroom walls, we are surrounded by colors that influence our mood, energy level, creativity, and overall well-being. Richard Webster offers an astonishing number of ways to use stimulating reds, soothing blues, and every other color of the rainbow to our advantage.

Webster begins with an overall picture of each color's major aspects—its psychological influence, healing qualities, emotional impact, and magical characteristics. From there, readers learn a multitude of color-based techniques involving astrology, the aura, candle magic, chakras, color rituals, crystals and gemstones, feng shui, flower magic, mandalas, meditation, numerology, and visualization. Webster demonstrates how color can be used to attract good luck, heal illness, reduce stress, create harmony in the home, overcome depression, solve problems, and magically enhance one's life in a variety of ways.

978-0-7387-0886-7
264 pages

$12.95

To order, call 1-877-NEW-WRLD
Prices subject to change without notice

Magical Symbols of Love & Romance
RICHARD WEBSTER

A candlelight dinner, wine, and roses are obvious choices when you want to woo a special someone. But that is only the tip of a colossal heart-shaped iceberg when it comes to expressing love and creating romance.

From pearls to pomegranates, tulips to truffles, vodka to Venus, Richard Webster introduces a wide array of items that signify this ubiquitous, complicated emotion. Going back to prehistoric cave paintings, Greek and Roman myth, and the origin of Valentine's Day, Webster offers a colorful history of love rituals, spells, charms, and aphrodisiacs. Modern success stories illustrate how individuals have used these powerful symbols to attract a partner, stimulate marriage, or resolve relationship issues. A handy reference and practical guide rolled into one, this book also advises you about how to use these symbols in your own life.

978-0-7387-1032-7
240 pages

$12.95

To order, call 1-877-NEW-WRLD
Prices subject to change without notice

Praying with Angels
RICHARD WEBSTER

Reverence for angels spans culture, faith, and time. But can these celestial messengers answer our prayers?

Praying with Angels can help you develop a rewarding, lifelong relationship with these divine creatures. From prayer to dreamwork, you'll explore a myriad of simple ways to communicate with angels. There are practical exercises and meditations to aid in developing angel awareness—an important first step towards angelic communication. Webster also provides a fascinating tour of the angelic kingdom, revealing the role and strengths of guardian angels, angels of the zodiac, elemental angels, and others. This crucial information lays the groundwork to help you select the appropriate angel to contact according to your unique circumstances. *Praying with Angels* also includes rituals and techniques for requesting healing, protection, abundance, and personal guidance.

978-0-7387-1098-3
240 pages

$13.95